MUSINGS OF A MODERATE

Musings of a Moderate

POLITICAL DISCOURSE IN THE AGE OF POLARIZATION

JORDAN R. BROWN

Palmetto Publishing Group
Charleston, SC

Musings of a Moderate

First Edition

Printed in the United States

Hardcover: 978-1-64112-031-9
Paperback: 978-1-64111-946-7
eBook: 978-1-64111-947-4

CONTENTS

Introduction

Being independent is a function of critical analysis, healthy skepticism, and political identity founded on the principles of kindness and reason. Independent thinkers are not merely frustrated partisans seeking a more ambiguous ideology, but rather intellectuals who refuse to allow a political litmus test to dictate their allegiance. The nature of independent politics requires candidates to be considered regardless of party, so individuals with positive intent and a focus on public service have the opportunity to serve in a community-oriented capacity. The United States of America is in desperate need of an antirevolution. This country deserves a deep breath and requires the calming force of moderation to mend the political divide. Opposing sides of the ideological spectrum demand an identical level of hysteria, blind allegiance, and willing suspension of disbelief from their supporters. The criticisms that are leveled in either direction are as ironic and contradictory as a Senate hearing on ethics. Republicans and Democrats have not, and possibly will never, realize that their animosity and ill-conceived policy ambitions are emphasizing the appeal of cooperation in politics. As the truth becomes a fleeting remnant of our imagination, it is time to move forward with policies that are effective and candidates who are transformational. We live in a time of limitless potential, where diversity and the open exchange of ideas will become our strength rather than a source of endless division.

From a practical perspective, independent thinking can become a welcome reprieve from the political hysteria that exists in modern American politics. Instead of individuals assessing facts and data as they become available, opinions are increasingly formulated based on social media trends and behavioral nudges intended to create specific overreactions with the hope that policy makers will relent to the manufactured pressure. Each person has the right to form partnerships or seek ideological harmony with their party or policy issue of choice, but the prevalence of groupthink and intellectual laziness is a dangerous pattern when the stakes are so high. Individuals should use their own unique political perspective to diversify the range of opinions and not allow themselves to be used as a conduit for party manipulation. Encouraging individual engagement through the development of unique preferences will decentralize advocacy coalitions, which have become the modern iteration of lobbying firms. The diffusion of perspectives and opinions will prevent the political and social fever pitch that makes for great headlines but leads to hastily passed policy initiatives that have a higher probability of unintended negative consequences in the future. Independent thinking is a necessity in a functioning democracy, and the pivot toward critical analysis begins by questioning assumptions and relying on verified data to start formulating an accurate opinion.

It is also essential to maintain a sense of self-awareness where each individual who chooses to engage in a political discussion can recognize that no matter how comfortable they feel in their analysis, an opinion can always be found in error as new information becomes available. A willingness to accept or at least acknowledge new information is yet another critical thinking skill that has been lost in the effort to win every argument. The political discourse does not have to be an adversarial collision of ideologies. When two people have a discussion, they are representing a personal perspective, not a party platform, yet when we aggregate all members in a debate, they suddenly become advocacy groups and lose their identity as individuals expressing an opinion. The aggregation of individual thoughts and ideas is merely the employment of a marketing device that allows campaign managers and media outlets to pander to the group they believe will be most receptive to their message. So far, people have been willing to align their unique identity with the group closest to their political persuasion, and the end result is the formation of policy silos that dissuade members from stepping outside the bounds of their rigid ideological preferences. Movement from a party or group allegiance to a system of free expression will reduce the likelihood of persistent negative interactions between individuals whose only contention is a difference of opinion. Being independent is the acceptance that others may have valid ideas and that critical thinking should take precedence over thought assimilation. Similarly, being independent is firmly believing that a variety of diverse opinions is not a risk to the democratic system but instead a threat to consolidated power that seeks to promote uniformity and dilute those who refuse to engage in divisive rhetoric.

CHAPTER 1

On Thoughts and Action

Few things are more comforting in a polarized political and social climate than to abandon reality in search of a victim who has been wronged by our opponents. While appreciating the struggles of others is a fundamentally human endeavor, the importance of full self-awareness is an equally admirable mental exercise. An endless deluge of movements, moments, and momentum cannot be so intense in our political will that we abandon the reality of our own lives. The scourge of racism, sexism, and prejudice on a myriad of issues can only be alleviated by the careful negotiation of idealism and reality. In the United States, all voices must be heard, but each individual voice is obscured in the pursuit of misplaced unity. What makes us unique, and allows the cure for social and political strife to be possible, is the selfish pursuit of our own aspirations. Decency and social tranquility are only available to those who represent their unique perspectives to the best of their abilities. Those who forgo their right to protest on behalf of their own grievances lose the passion and clarity to achieve the objectives that will generate necessary change effectively.

Modern activism is a dysfunctional appropriation of the emotions of others, without realizing that the personal experience of a human being is the only force sufficient to generate the will for change. No matter how grave the affront, we cannot save someone by sympathizing with their plight, but we can demonstrate our support by being true to ourselves for the betterment of society. Each of us is a more effective citizen when we focus on the issues that affect our daily lives and refrain from appropriating the struggle of others for political gain. Sustainable change is never a sprint, and no group is influential enough to enforce fairness and equality among all people. Justice and equality are figments of our cultural imagination and are not defined well enough to provide a sustained path toward social cohesion. The belief that we can carry an injustice from advocacy to extinction in the span of a news cycle is a misguided and naive assumption. The greatest achievement a person can make is to further their own cause far enough for the next generation to take the baton and complete the next leg of the race. The change we want for ourselves is possible for our children, but only if we remain focused and are driven by the appropriate intentions. It is the best elements within ourselves that are capable of propelling positive change a step closer to existence. Injustice should ignite fury, but that fury must be channeled and replaced with wisdom and patience to achieve any objective.

Some parts are small, and some are large, but every person should be respected for their contribution to progress. Advocating vehemently for a party or cause is a diversion from our duty to fight for the best interests of our family and work toward a more cooperative society. We cannot lose our individuality or personal ambition in search of belonging to a group bent on monopolizing on our insecurities. So rare is the case of absolute truth that it is a waste of time to disagree so fiercely with those who do not share our opinions. The benefit of moderation in thoughts and action is that arguments on either side are observed and considered clearly without the effect of blind emotion and persistent impatience. Careful examination and measured responses are our only recourse when society and politics demand our willful ignorance, perpetual rage, and unconditional loyalty.

CHAPTER 2
Abortion

Abortion is an issue that requires the utmost sensitivity and empathy to discuss. On one side of the debate are people who believe the legalization of the procedure is the foundation of equal rights for women. On the other side are people firm in their belief that the termination of a pregnancy at any stage is murder. When the arguments on both sides are diametrically opposed, the willing suspension of reactive anger is required to find common ground. Issues perceived as life and death rapidly descend into an unproductive war between ideologies; therefore, in this matter, the effective use of logic is vital to avoid further polarization.

As a legal matter, the issue of abortion is already considered settled law. The Supreme Court has ruled on the subject, and the likelihood of reversing legal precedent is exceedingly low unless politically motivated justices undermine the reproductive rights of women. Arguing for the elimination of abortion rights in the United States is the business of attorneys and religious organizations seeking to sustain their careers by manipulating the pocketbook of misguided evangelicals. Additionally, it is unwise to overturn *Roe v. Wade* because many women face difficult, and sometimes impossible, circumstances that lead them to have the procedure. For these women, it is essential for safe and clean facilities to be available. However, a political discussion on abortion should include treating the root of the problem. Abortion is merely one symptom of a more substantial societal flaw where we refuse to create effective programs that care for women facing difficult circumstances.

To effectively reduce abortion, sexual education in the school system needs to be updated and improved to provide accurate and relevant information for adolescents. Public schools should have a curriculum that promotes safety, addresses risk, and clearly defines the issue of consent to empower teens to take full control of their sexual health and avoid potentially unforeseen consequences. The school districts should also make contraceptives readily accessible by placing a qualified medical professional within each school district to write prescriptions and provide relevant information to young women who may not have access to a general practitioner or gynecologist to receive birth control. Reducing the incidence of unplanned pregnancy is dependent on the development of effective educational programs and contraceptive resources being discreetly available to sexually active adolescents.

For adult women who require additional resources and assistance, a community-based clinic with a mentorship component would provide a legitimate alternative to abortion if they seek information on a variety of potential options. Such programs must be an effective public-private partnership and would serve as an excellent funding opportunity for foundations, individual philanthropists, and federal and state agencies. Supporting women, rather than constraining their choices, should be the focus of organizations that seek to reduce the number of abortions in the United States. Women should have the freedom to choose, but they should also have the information to decide the best path forward based on a full array of options. Some support systems are in place in a few communities, but for many women, the choice to carry a pregnancy to term creates additional uncertainty and severe financial consequences. Providing long-term support mechanisms throughout the country will guarantee that a child will be well supported rather than considered a potential personal or career liability.

The unique aspect of the proposed program is to provide funding for additional social workers who are specially trained to mentor and guide new mothers through the pregnancy and the first years of the child's life. The clinics will then provide excellent prenatal and postnatal care for the mother, and the necessary psychological and emotional support for the entire family after the baby is born. The social workers will also reduce the potential financial risk of keeping babies by helping women apply for the many programs that already exist to assist women and young children. The mentors can help women navigate applications for Medicaid, SNAP benefits, and ABC vouchers for affordable childcare. Maximizing the support structures already in place is an essential tool for assisting women in improving their circumstances when they face the crisis of an unplanned pregnancy. Another critical aspect of the proposed strategy is to provide priority access for children in the program to first-step early childhood education resources. Every child deserves a quality education, but it is vital to ensure that early intervention programs are available to the highest-risk students. There is no need to continue allowing children born under challenging circumstances to become further statistics without doing all that is possible to improve their future. It is more pragmatic for the focus of public policy to be on the improvement of education and essential resources for children and families than to try addressing the problems via the criminal justice system when at-risk children enter adulthood. The benefit to society and the American economy lies in the ability to help children become college graduates rather than inmates. An investment of resources for each family will yield returns for generations to come.

Women should always have the right to choose, but that choice should no longer be between terminating a pregnancy or suffering from an increased likelihood of poverty and social isolation. Pregnant women must have a full range of possible options, including ending a pregnancy or raising a child with the support of their community and access to all the resources any affluent family would have at their disposal. Focusing on the choice between life and death is an effective diversion from the issues that affect the reproductive decision-making process. It is time to support and respect women without using them as political devices and make sure resources are available to provide a safe and supportive environment in the event of either an abortion or a full-term birth.

CHAPTER 3

Banks

Banks are the leviathans that reap financial rewards by pilfering the crumbs of dignity left to the poor. The banking system has become a complex network of algorithms in which the purposeful exclusion of the underclass is delegated to a computer and regurgitated by a banker who has been stripped of their autonomy through the implementation of impersonal corporate policies. Rather than providing a mechanism for economic mobility, banks have become a symbol of American inequality, and they are utterly impervious to the real consequences their actions have on the lives of average people. We often repeat the adage that America is the land of opportunity, but for the vast majority of people, the opportunities that were once possibilities to securing stable financial futures have dissolved into distant memories.

Rather than striving to meet the needs of customers from all socio-economic backgrounds, banks have found additional sources of revenue by exploiting the growing divide between the rich and poor. The working-class people who face the prospect of negative account balances each morning represent no more than a minor nuisance when they enter the bank to inquire as to why overdraft fees have left them with a seemingly insurmountable shortfall. The hard decisions, such as paying a bill beyond the current account balance to make ends meet, has now created a deficit equaling half the next paycheck and threatens to push another hardworking American family closer to financial calamity. Week after week, the same process is repeated with stomach-churning certainty. Meanwhile, the political leaders and activists who claim they fight for the interests of everyday Americans have themselves forgotten the feeling of a negative account balance mostly comprised of fees applied by the bank, and the inherent sense of helplessness when no one is listening to your plea for fairness and empathy. For the leaders who claim they share our interests, banks are a source of campaign contributions, mortgage loans, and a friendly smile every time they enter a branch and the teller views their balance on the screen. For the rest of us, we are locked out of a system that benefits a few at the expense of the majority. The common bond of ordinary people is not access to home loans and affordable financing, but instead being told a hold has been placed on the check we needed to buy groceries for dinner.

We must remember that inequality does not necessarily stem from the people who pay us but rather the people who take our money. Banks have a system that requires our participation to function in the modern economy, and they have an efficient way to profit from our hardship. Those of us living paycheck to paycheck are subjected to the whims of executives who have no concern beyond their bottom line. Reorganizing transactions to maximize the number of overdraft fees is an exploitative practice that is a game to banks, but it represents an incredible burden for millions of American families. Ironically, banks also spend part of their profits earned through depleting the accounts of those living in the margins on philanthropic endeavors that benefit the poor to alter our perception of their corporate responsibility. Rather than redistributing the income of the needy account holder to

the needy stranger, they should consider alleviating the harmful practices that push millions of us each month into a perilous position of
desperation and hopelessness. Access to loans and financial resources
that provide equal opportunities for upward mobility would be nice;
however, in our current condition, we would be happy to merely see
an end to the regularly scheduled raids on our checking accounts that
intentionally monopolize on our inherent lack of leverage to advocate
on our behalf.

CHAPTER 4

On a Sound Mind

A sound mind is achieved by working intentionally each day to increase our patience and wisdom. People are undoubtedly good, but the experiences that shape our personalities can distort the naturally positive aspects of the human spirit if we do not seek personal growth and appreciate the value of introspection. All of us carry the burden of inequality, despair, and anger, yet we still maintain the ability within our character to determine the way each experience shapes our lives. The negativity can help us evolve into more positive and productive versions of ourselves, or we can allow our experiences to consume the glimmers of hope that exist within all of us.

The current national pastime is espousing a doctrine of division aimed at anyone we deem worthy of our rage. The virtue of patience has been lost to an expectation of immediate gratification, and the tranquility of contentment has been replaced with an overwhelming resentment. The lost joy derived from the simplicity of existence is eroding our proclivity for kindness and understanding. The mind is chaotic, and life is turbulent; nevertheless, we prefer to project our defects onto others and hate them instead of ourselves. Suddenly, reality is turned upside down so we can mask our shortcomings in the confusion of progress. Similarly, when we fail to attain the American Dream in its various forms, we prefer to imagine hidden obstacles where they do not exist to avoid responsibility for the consequences of our own choices. Moral indignancy and social outrage are clever disguises, but the condition of the mind cannot improve through the development of an alternate reality in which relativity becomes a blanket justification for any behavior.

The answer to our problem is the deafening silence that forces us to find peace with ourselves. Kind words have been cast aside, and the hateful rhetoric is reaching its pinnacle. The only alternative we have when harsh words sink gently in an ocean of rage is to focus our thoughts and actions on improving the world in which we live. The institutions on which society exists are being mercilessly destroyed by all sides of the political spectrum and along each step of the social hierarchy. If the institutions are genuinely insufficient to serve the needs of modern society, then we should be even more determined to use the cognitive tool of a sound mind to build a better world. We can destroy the cornerstones of our nation, or we can work to ensure that further construction includes all the fixtures of tolerance, prosperity, and self-determination. Anger alone will not bear the fruits we intend to grow.

CHAPTER 5

Campaigning

Elections have become a demonstration of unapologetic narcissism rather than a presentation of substantive policy. The thirsts for power and superfluous titles have caused the voting public to become an afterthought, and this is no more evident than in campaign finance. Campaigns do not become corrupt merely because corporations or wealthy benefactors attempt to influence leaders with donations. The real corruption lies in the necessity to spend without presenting a coherent platform. Millions of Americans choose to support candidates they believe will represent their interests, but the impact of individual donations from the average working-class citizen is negligible.

Many candidates who choose to run for public office receive donations from questionable sources, and they take out loans to finance their campaigns in amounts well beyond the anticipated stipend or salary for the position should they win. How in good conscience does a bank deny a home loan to a hardworking family yet happily provide loans to political candidates with no guarantee they will be elected? Furthermore, how is a loan secured for a position that pays a fraction of the amount borrowed? The corruption we know pales in comparison to the advantages provided to politicians from sources that remain hidden from public view.

Campaigns should be exercises in democracy in which each candidate presents their policy proposals, and those with the best ideas are supported by the people with both their votes and monetary contributions. Fairness becomes a faint remnant of idealistic naivete when the candidate with the most money and weakest policy acumen continues to garner the highest number of votes. Campaigning has become the playground of the manipulative rather than the platform for intelligent discussion and policy development. The power vested in the political elite has ultimately remained intact, even though we can see the deceit and corruption in plain view and feel helpless to stop the progression. The cancer of money in campaigns has metastasized, and we are not sure where to operate first. The problem cannot be pinpointed any longer and is not caused by a single individual or corporation seeking to interfere with the public's right to choose their representatives.

A wholesale change in campaign finance is the only way to treat the disease that is quickly creeping throughout our democracy and threatens to snuff out our last twinge of enthusiasm for the election process. First, candidates for congressional and state elections should only be permitted to collect donations within their state. This will help eliminate the surge of contributions from across the country that enable manipulation in key elections. Second, no candidate should be able to take out a loan to help fund a campaign. In a democratic republic, it is essential candidates for office be heard in equal measure, and the field should be narrowed according to competency, not credit score. Third, ballots in all elections should not list the party affiliation of the candidates. Too many candidates avoid having to produce a legitimate vision for the future of the nation by taking advantage of districts with a preponderance of either Democrat or Republican voters. The end result is an electorate so blinded by party affiliation that a child could win in a landslide as long as they have the correct party designation beside their name.

Shifting to a system in which policy superiority and professional competence prevails over all other variables would restore sanity to the election process and force campaigns to be focused and lean. Also, the prevalence of bank loans and outside contributions should be recognized as a tactic of manipulation to propel the best-connected candidate ahead of the potential leaders with real visions for the future. If the correct steps are taken, the election process can become an equitable meritocracy instead of its current form as a predetermined obligation for autocrats.

CHAPTER 6

Campus Reform

Colleges were initially intended to be havens of higher education, career training, and social identity development, but recent trends have quickly moved toward the normalization of debauchery and underachievement. The college administrators are happy to oblige the students who enroll for the mystical "college experience," and have little regard for the rapid erosion of academic standards and campus safety. Thousands of students in each state attend college for the binge drinking, risky sexual behavior, and comradery; all the while their interest in course offerings is limited to whichever classes are known for the most lenient grade distribution. The supposedly valuable experience of a four-year party bridging childhood and adulthood has succeeded in conjuring a certain allure among young people, but the result has impugned the sterling reputation of the institutions they attend.

The amount of violence, the number of sexual assaults, and pervasiveness of destructive drug and alcohol abuse are impossible to quantify accurately. The institutions can only provide information on reported instances of problematic or abusive behavior, and they have clear incentives to sweep negative publicity under the proverbial rug.

Because universities do not want to present accurate portrayals of their campus environments, they have made a habit of consistently turning a blind eye to the numerous daily violations of school policies and laws.

Simple reforms are needed to ensure that colleges remain safe places for parents to send their children and to protect the value of the academic experience as tuition rates continue to rise. Currently, campus police are either complicit in the lax policies of the administrators, or they are woefully understaffed and overwhelmed. The easiest way to quickly reduce the number of sexual assaults, alcohol-related deaths, and violence is to enforce the drinking age on and around campus every night. Merely applying the laws, which should already be a top priority for universities that are responsible for the health and well-being of thousands of students, would immediately restore some semblance of peace and sanity to the college community. We have entirely abandoned our fundamental responsibilities to teach, encourage, and mentor as ways to thwart systemic dysfunction, and the leadership teams are too concerned about growing enrollment and revenues to care for the students who are already attending.

Fraternities and sororities are yet further examples of the contrived traditions that have subverted the mission of higher education. Colleges are forced to expend resources to control the chaos within Greek-letter organizations, and even so, they have little knowledge of the extent of the problem represented by immaturity combined with all the vices available on campus. Because of the continuous examples of lawless and dangerous behavior, universities interested in upholding the original missions of their institutions should consider eliminating Greek-letter organizations. All the authorities on campus need to do for the fraternities and sororities to collapse is enforce the drinking age and make sure claims of sexual assault are thoroughly investigated and prosecuted to the fullest extent of the law. Partnerships between campus authorities and city or state law enforcement agencies would be useful tools of deterrence among young people who have seemingly decided legal standards of conduct are not applicable within the scope of the college experience.

Campus reform to curb destructive behavior is not a selective attack on fun but rather a set of straightforward changes that will help reduce the number of young people whose lives are irreparably harmed by the normalized malaise. If universities want us to believe they take sexual assault seriously, then they should be fully committed to correcting some of the underlying problems that may lead to a young person becoming the target of violence. There will be far fewer claims of inebriated confusion resulting in a lack of consent when the law is enforced, and students who violate the rules are treated as adults rather than children enjoying their newfound freedom at a highly overpriced day-care facility. The institutional mission of intellectual development should never be diminished or impeded by the continual incompetence of administrators who preach standards while inviting depravity.

CHAPTER 7
On Activism

It is increasingly evident that activism is rarely executed without devolving into a destructive pattern of critical moralizing. The greatest asset we possess is the ability to analyze our current conditions critically and correctly identify problems in our collective patterns of behavior. The genesis of change is the active pursuit of a new set of objectives, but the best course of action does not have to include mutual vitriol for ideological opponents. Our inability to appreciate the differences of opinion we have is a symptom of generational immaturity and in no way indicates that we are becoming proficient at constructing persuasive arguments. Tradition and behavioral norms dictated individual development when our country was still primarily a monolithic society. Increased diversity and the pursuit of equal rights for historically disenfranchised groups have precipitated a reckoning between the past and the present. The evolution of our collective identity requires activism to implement a new ideological lens. However, the prevalence of hate and anger as a debate strategy reveals that neither side in many arguments possesses the intellectual or emotional maturity to identify the best method of advocacy and implementation.

While it is a positive development that we have begun to address difficult issues at hand, we must acknowledge our deficiencies in formulating sustainable solutions. Our duty is not to solve any problems but instead to embrace our proclivity for critical thinking and creative analysis, and to use our skills to identify the correct starting point for future generations to solve the most complex and urgent problems. The hateful rhetoric that has become synonymous with the national dialogue on a variety of issues is nothing more than the expression of our frustration and a symptom of weary minds. We should not be disheartened from the lack of productivity within our discussions, because the achievement of our generation lies within the fearless pursuit of intangible objectives. We are seeking to change minds and build a more equitable society for an increasingly diverse population. The work in front of us requires wisdom and patience, not an insistence on becoming the loudest voice in the echo chamber of change.

The future depends on our ability to reconcile our historical significance with the objectives we would like to accomplish. We cannot declare our time and place to be significant if all we contribute is the erosion of decency. This generation cannot force permanent change in an environment where the free expression of ideas is the cornerstone of our democracy, but we do have the ability to inspire the continued pursuit of human evolution in the generations to come. If we resist the urge to scream change into fruition, we have a better opportunity to instill the values we hold dear into the minds of our children. From time to time, a collection of people must sacrifice the battle to win the war of ideological progress. When we rely on militant advocacy to present a new perspective, we relinquish the power of sound arguments as the basis for mass appeal, thereby undermining the very purpose of activism. The alternative to our current discourse is to embrace the tranquility of compromise and allow whichever cause we choose to pursue to gain a foothold an inch at a time. No issue is ever solved with a single rally, march, or presidential election. What we must realize is that sustainable change requires popular support and that a majority of Americans will always be reticent to embrace change that is created through an authoritarian insistence of blind acceptance. Support for a cause is the first step toward change, but passion is far better than rage as a tool of persuasion.

CHAPTER 8
Climate Change

Climate change has mutated from a constructive discussion of industrial stewardship to an ideological battle over the survival of civilization. The truth is that we fully understand the importance of protecting the environment and intentionally taking steps to mitigate the effects of industrialization and global population growth. However, suggesting the consequences of global development will result in irreversible environmental destruction is an exaggerated attempt to control the public discourse with logical fallacies and far-fetched predictions. Insisting on espousing the inevitability of collapse and human extinction, no matter how forceful the appeal, will only inspire skepticism. A more reasonable tone that incorporates the interests of individuals, supports the economic growth required to support a large population, and monopolizes shared environmental concerns would garner far more popular support.

The constant focus on the United States as the primary contributor to pollution and environmental destruction ignores the significant effect of pollutants created through unrestrained industrialization in nations such as China and India. Activists have become reliant on sympathetic ears rather than requiring accountability from the most recent perpetrators of environmental negligence. Those who would condemn the average person for utilizing the benefits of technological and economic development to improve their quality of life are exploiting the low-hanging fruit of consumerism to sustain their movement. Actions to reverse the course of climate change must include challenging the industrial practices of nations with zero tolerance for dissent and protest. Activism within the confines of freedom, along with significant ideological agreement, is more of an opportunity for self-aggrandizement than an actual mechanism for change. All nations should be accountable for responsible development, but the current advocacy environment seems focused on limiting the economic capacity of the United States to the detriment of the American people. Garnering support for policy initiatives that address climate change must be inclusive and equitable. Otherwise, such efforts will never hold any weight with the general public and will always be viewed as a disproportional punishment resulting from postindustrial retrospection.

Climate-change policies also have the potential of maintaining global inequality by restricting industrial development in nations that have yet to build the capacity for economic expansion. In fact, there may be no more cringeworthy example of white privilege than reaping all the benefits of industrialization and then insisting other nations pursue cost-prohibitive alternatives. Our egocentric pursuit of environmental redemption places a tremendous burden on developing countries that desperately need to harness the power of efficient industrialization to emerge from poverty and become an integral part of the global economy. We cannot continue to operate under the assumption that economic development is dangerous when billions of people continue to suffer from an unimaginable deficit of essential resources.

Every nation can learn from the past mistakes of industrialization and the real environmental consequences of indiscriminate development, but that does not give us the right to dictate the pathways for economic growth other countries must follow. The mere discussion of climate change and environmentalism is a product of academic and scientific development that is directly provided by the efficiency of our economic system. Without industrialization, we would be hoping our food supply would sustain us through a harsh winter rather than pontificating on the existential threat of climate change at a local coffee shop. Let us not be so blind to the plight of others that we insist on restrictive global policies that force developing nations to bear the burdens of our mistakes.

Climate change and the continual degradation of our natural world are serious concerns that require a thoughtful policy response. Gradual reductions in emissions and the eventual elimination of single-use products that pollute the environment are worthwhile goals. However, such measures do not have the luxury of thwarting the standard policy-development process. Climate-change measures do not currently enjoy widespread support because they are draconian and often lack a feasible path toward responsible implementation. Public skepticism is falsely characterized as a national aversion to scientific data, but it is instead an aversion to unilateral action that threatens the economic growth we all depend on to prosper. Dissent should not be viewed as an obstacle to environmental protection but rather as an opportunity to develop better solutions that will ultimately garner majority support. The American political system is unique because bad ideas do not become acceptable when an issue is declared an emergency. There is no shortcut created by militant fervor. A policy is still required to be thorough, thoughtful, and feasible before it garners the support necessary to become law.

CHAPTER 9
Criminal Justice

The fundamental axiom of our criminal justice system is an enthusiastic commitment to the idea that the accused are innocent until proven guilty. No person should be permitted to exist above the law, and no person should be forced to become a victim of the law due to their socioeconomic vulnerability. The values of jurisprudence can never be abandoned to fit a specific political narrative that will disrupt the long-term integrity of the justice system. The principles that ensure fairness and the equitable distribution of justice for all people are not an ambiguous pledge subject to interpretation for the benefit of social evolution or political expediency. No matter how heinous the crime might be, we cannot in good conscience abscond from the presumption of innocence that allows us to live with the security and knowledge that our freedom is held in the highest regard. Prosecution should not be used as a tool of terror, nor should it be wielded as a weapon to perpetuate racial oppression. A fair criminal justice system treats all people with the respect of assumed innocence and treats them humanely if convicted.

The United States gains its strength from the existence of a justice system that provides a safe and stable environment for economic activity and social cooperation. However, the inconsistencies in the enforcement of laws have created a dichotomy of injustice for those in poverty. Without the financial resources to find adequate representation, thousands of people are convicted of crimes and sentenced to prison terms in circumstances in which someone with moderate means to afford competent representation would have been able to either prove their innocence or secure a lesser sentence. The use of plea bargaining has evolved from a policy that benefits the accused based on evidence, to a catalyst for docket clearing in an overwhelmed system. While plea bargaining may expedite justice in the interest of taxpayers and the accused, when it becomes a tool of coercion, the bargain ceases to represent the original intent of prosecutorial autonomy. Justice, no matter how slow the wheels may turn in our incarceration-obsessed system, must always be the highest priority for the individuals in charge of protecting the most sacred element of our social contract.

The first step in the process of reform is to rectify past mistakes. African Americans and other racial, ethnic, or socioeconomic groups who have been adversely impacted by the unbalanced distribution of punishment should have their sentences adjusted to reflect a renewed commitment to the abolishment of discrimination. Furthermore, individuals accused of nonviolent crimes should be considered eligible for suspended sentences if convicted, thereby reducing the problems associated with overcrowding. Clearing the congested dockets must also be a high priority for criminal justice reform. Plea bargaining is a useful tool, but it cannot be a legal crutch from which overzealous prosecutors avoid exposing the inherent weakness of a case while still achieving a conviction. Reducing a charge from patently absurd to mildly reasonable is not a bargain for the individuals who lack the resources to advocate effectively on their behalf.

In the end, the justice system should be restored to the original intent of objectively determining guilt from innocence. Racial injustice and coercion have always been a part of the system, but justice, in theory, is the evenhanded enforcement of the law without regard for the potential biases of critical stakeholders. The pure interpretation of justice is the one for which we must dedicate our efforts for reform. A system in which innocence is assumed, and guilt is only achieved through the presentation of evidence beyond a reasonable doubt, might be a difficult pursuit in a country where every participant is imbued with their presuppositions and prejudices. Despite the difficulty, pursuing perfection must always be the starting point on the path toward justice. Millions of Americans stand to benefit from a renewed appreciation and understanding of the concept of *innocent until proven guilty.*

While the passage of targeted criminal justice reforms may be politically feasible, it is important to understand that no part of the justice system operates independently of the other. When an investigation is mishandled, the consequences flow downstream and contaminate the remaining elements of due process. An ill-tempered or racially insensitive police officer, an overzealous prosecutor, a judge basking in the glory of moral superiority, and a jury deliberately nullifying the law are all potential pitfalls for the accused when a targeted policy proposal ignores the necessity of holistic reform. Criminal justice reform requires a commitment to improving the operational aspects of the system from the first point of contact through the appeals process. Justice is thwarted when the underprivileged live in constant fear of being devoured by the very system that has been constructed to protect their interests.

CHAPTER 10
On Authority

No person has dominion over another or the inherent power to decide the fate of a free man or woman. Those considered to be in positions of authority are merely people with title, and in no way od they have legitimate value above others in a cultural hierarchy. The power derived from certain occupations should be limited, closely monitored, and exercised with extreme caution. No force is more corrupting than the imposition of authority based on the assumption of power or superiority. Authority itself is a collectively imposed subversion of liberty, and abuse is inevitable when equality becomes a matter of opinion rather than a fundamental truth. Reducing the stranglehold of authority is superfluous in a country where people operate under the false assumption that justice is blind and freedom is provided to all people in equal measure. A fight against authority is no more than a struggle against a ghost that threatens to take your liberty with no recourse. The powerful understand that justice is blind to them, but they often remove their blindfolds to take aim at the powerless and those who seek to limit their influence.

Respect must flow into every crevasse of the social structure; otherwise, our interactions will become emblematic of a destructive caste system that limits social and economic mobility and imposes the will of the few on the many. How we conceive of power, and the pace with which we begin to disregard the supposition of authority, will directly coincide with the nature of our interpersonal relationships. Inequity is born of the proclivity for suspicion and fear between the socioeconomic classes. When the rich believe the poor will squander the power of authority, and the poor believe the rich are using their influence to suppress the opportunity for upward mobility, the only bridge between the two is conflict. A revised assessment of value and human potential is required to decipher the criminals from the righteous and the leaders from the scoundrels. Too often, the current hierarchy is used to confuse the characteristics that make us all equal and pursue any means to prevent the underprivileged from ascending. The foundation of trust between the classes has been irreparably damaged, but a new relationship built on the fair exchange of ideas and labor for monetary gain is the best chance we have to mend the divide caused by past transgressions.

Creating an American meritocracy is a worthwhile idea to ponder but has the potential to unveil an entirely new set of problematic conditions. The first issue is deciding who would determine the definition of merit. Surely those in power who have convinced the unsuspecting that they possess authority in a literal sense would not delegate the transition toward an equitable system to the people who have been negatively impacted by the corrupting influence of hierarchical power. Instead, those who have seized control from a perverse sense of authority would feel compelled to exercise their superiority by creating new social and economic structures that appease the struggling masses yearning to gain nothing more than a stable footing. The result would not be the orderly transition to a meritocracy but rather a strategic realignment that elongates the hierarchy while leaving the same individuals at the top.

For liberty to be sustainable, the notion of authority, either inherited or appropriated, must be vanquished. Additionally, the power that accompanies job titles or scholarly achievement should be used to build bridges rather than walls. The distribution of power is sometimes random but is usually concentrated within a distinct lineage and not available to those deemed unworthy in the purview of the powerful. The hope for our future and sustaining the principles of American exceptionalism is that money and power will no longer be the sole indicators of success and instead become ancillary benefits of making the American Dream a possibility to all people. In the end, the assumption of superiority derived from authority is an absurd notion in a country where we consider all people to be created equal.

Furthermore, the significance of power in our society has two distinct paths of operation. Power can be used as it is currently: to restrict access to the opportunities and resources theoretically available to every American. Alternatively, power can be used as the platform from which good people hold out their hands and begin to provide opportunities for the suppressed voices to speak loudly and clearly so the rest of the people can feel empowered to reach their full potential.

Once again, we face the tedious and challenging reality that effective change begins with a new perspective within the home and then spreads very slowly over the span of generations from a single house, to a single community, to a single state, to a single country, and eventually far beyond the borders of any nation. While the prospect of an arduous process to alleviate the oppression of authority and the corruption of power is daunting, the way in which the world evolves reinforces our belief that the key to change always lies within the mind of a single individual. Incremental change is how we systematically expand the notion of equality, and a continuing commitment to social and cultural evolution will allow each generation to impose its definition of equity within our society.

CHAPTER 11

Deportation

Current deportation policy is a confluence of bad ideas working together to destroy the moral fabric of the United States and divide families to suit the whims of a political minority. There is no basis according to our modern definition of human rights and collective moral conscience for removing residents who pose no physical threat to citizens. The fact that we would tolerate such a violation of human rights and decency exemplifies our preference to ignore problems that do not pose direct threats to our quality of life as American citizens. While we stare at our devices and consume our minds with endless distractions, good people are being ripped from their families and delivered to squalor in countries they risked their lives to escape in the first place. Mass deportation is not a complex moral problem, because it is clear that current policies are an abandonment of our core values as a melting pot of culture founded on the ideals of hard work and unrelenting freedom.

The presumption of lawlessness is no longer a legitimate reason to turn our open arms into clenched fists to shield our prosperity from the rest of the world. Contrived charges are the norm for immigrants; meanwhile, citizens with enough wealth to buy their freedom continue to evade accountability in the judicial system. In America, the scales of justice seem to be a measurement of wealth rather than an indicator of truth. Unlawful presence and presenting false documentation are manufactured justifications for ill treatment, yet they are merely the result of existence for those who desperately seek safety and security within our borders. A child brought to this country for refuge must be differentiated from criminals who ignore the law to wreak havoc within our borders.

Deportation should be a mechanism for exporting severe threats to national security, not a political device to be deployed when ideologues demand their pound of flesh. The dangerous residents who commit heinous crimes or associate with dangerous criminal gangs should be the target of the full weight of the US government. Excluded from the chaotic and heart-wrenching nature of being hunted by the authorities should be the families who violate no liberties of others on their journeys to a better life. Addressing the rights of Dreamers alone will not suffice when the human toll is so high and continues to grow each day. Immigrants, from any nation with any legal status, should not be above the law, but they do not deserve to be considered as beneath the law either. An immigrant should have the same rights as a citizen who works daily to live a good life and provide an opportunity for their children to experience a safe and prosperous future. No person should ever be deported from this country when they live and work peacefully, especially when the alternative in their country of origin is a life of brutality and poverty. Our goal as Americans is to spread the gift of freedom and economic opportunity, not hold it as a birthright reserved for citizens.

CHAPTER 12
Drug Crisis

The rampant drug abuse in the United States remains the quiet crisis that is only a topic of conversation during a slow news day. Despite our preference to ignore the effects of the growing problem of narcotics, we cannot stand aside while the scourge of addiction destroys millions of families. It is time to treat the drug crisis like a disease in need of a cure and begin allocating public and private resources accordingly. Yes, addiction traditionally starts with a series of poor choices, but the proliferation of prescription medications containing addictive opioids is beginning to blur the line between junkie and victim.

Our commitment to developing effective treatment programs is dismal and reflects the attention span of a citizenry that is always eager to find a new crisis before the previous one is solved. If as many people died fighting in a war overseas as have succumbed to drug overdoses, there would be a national outcry for answers and solutions. Instead, because the alleged "junkie" is a natural outlet for judgment and ridicule, we make minimal effort to quell the growing problem. Treatment programs must be available to everyone who needs help with substance abuse. And we need to provide the research and development funding to discover new treatments that go far beyond the resuscitation cycle. First responders are forced to fight a battle against addiction, one dose of Narcan at a time. We should be embarrassed that we have delegated the responsibility of the health and well-being of our vulnerable citizens to emergency medical personnel who are helpless to treat the underlying mental and physical issues that lead to abuse.

Every possible remedy should be explored and implemented where possible. Controlling the flow of narcotics across the northern and southern borders is a matter of national security and is a requirement if we are to begin mitigating the problem at the source. Also, the legalization of medical marijuana in all fifty states needs to be a priority so that alternative pain management techniques can replace or supplement opioid prescriptions. There must also be a commitment to expanding the capacity of treatment centers. Attaining sobriety is the ultimate test of willpower, and the process is significantly more difficult for individuals who plead for help in overcoming their addictions and are met with financial impediments or lack of space at facilities in their community. Considering the strength of our national economic position, there is no reason why an addict who wants to achieve sobriety should be denied access to the necessary resources. The pleas of the affected can no longer fall on deaf ears just because we have moved on to the next headline. Our people and their safety and well-being take precedence over the litany of superfluous distractions that occupy our attention.

We cannot afford inaction against the effects of drug abuse. The violence that erupts from the illegal drug trade continues to claim the lives of innocent people. And the safety concerns that arise are quickly eroding the social and economic fabric of our nation. Additionally, the costs associated with the growing problem of addiction will far outweigh the investment we make in a permanent, multifaceted solution.

The health-care system is pushed to the brink, and first responders are fighting a war of attrition against addicts and dealers who are always searching for new ways to circumvent the law. Combined, we have a picture of dysfunction that prevents us from realizing the full extent of our economic capacity and social progress. At the crossroads of our moral obligations, there is no room for indecision and no excuse for continuing to fail our people when they desperately need a helping hand.

CHAPTER 13
On Commonality

The fundamental principle of decency is seemingly lost on this generation. We share in the same human experience that should lead us to unite, yet despite our similarities, we search for a cacophony of reasons to be divided. Political rhetoric and tribal allegiance distort our common goals and erase the notion that our opinions may be wrong. None of us make our journey through life without trouble, difficulty, contentment, joy, success, and failure, but we waste our time convincing ourselves that our particular path is superior to that of another. The bonds of humanity are broken, and there is seemingly no way to mend our differences. We are caught in an endless cycle of futile conflict, with a constant desire to make others suffer so that we might experience the illusion of political dominance.

Social harmony slips further out of sight the more we rely on division and ridicule to achieve our policy objectives. Cooperation, not conflict, is the ideology of enlightenment and is the greatest hope we will all share for a future of peace and prosperity. Our lives are but a moment, yet we regularly make a habit of disregarding the opportunities we have to strengthen our social bonds and enhance the political process.

Faith, ideology, and belief are identifying characteristics that make each one of us uniquely suited to fulfill our purpose, but when they turn into fanatical dedication, they have the power to distort our sense of self and diminish the importance of diverse opinions. The characterization of opponents as ignorant and incompetent does not bolster the merit of our perspective. When the infallibility of our beliefs is reinforced in the vacuum of populism, it causes us to assume our logic is superior to another's. No matter how many headlines validate our perspective, good policy will never emerge from groupthink. Once we fail to recognize our own cognitive deficiencies, the need to silence the opinions of others becomes our sole motivation in all actions and dialogue. It is time we admit that all people are good, but we are hopelessly vulnerable to environmental influences that cause us to abandon the bond of humanity and seek to justify our means to achieve the desired end.

Our future can be defined by the ability to overcome the layers of collective scars that diminish our sense of community, or the future can be held hostage by the same biases and insecurities that have caused us to turn on our neighbors. It is up to us to decide the direction we prefer to follow. Wisdom and understanding are not forged through hostility and mistrust, but rather by the intensity of our commitment to remain kind and cooperative while existing in a flawed world. No one will tell us to make peace with ourselves and accept the equality of all people, but we will find a particularly humbling solace when our indignation slowly turns into an appreciation for the common road that we all navigate.

CHAPTER 14
Environmentalism

Amid an intense ideological battle over climate change, the concept of conservation has become an afterthought. Conservation is not a niche policy topic but rather a symbol of our national commitment to environmental stewardship. We need to appreciate that any serious climate policy begins with conservation, not the implementation of vague draconian strategies that are increasingly polarizing and cost-prohibitive for many businesses. In the political debate over the environment, garnering support for common-sense steps toward better stewardship of nature is much easier than implementing a series of new federal or international regulations. Environmental rehabilitation is facilitated by building a case for concrete individual actions that will, in turn, yield a significant collective benefit for our future.

Conservation is the bridge between political narratives that enables each person to take ownership of their environmental impact. Rather than focusing on extreme measures that have potentially severe economic consequences, and little popular support among voters, we should consider policy initiatives that are far less complicated and more actionable for the average person. People do not connect to climate science when their daily commute is labeled as a contributor to environmental degradation. Most families strive each day to work hard and make ends meet, and the endless stream of condescending lectures from activists and the political elite are viewed as direct attacks on the resources they need to achieve financial stability. We have forgotten that a successful policy initiative in a democracy is implemented from the bottom up, not the top down. Rather than insisting that people cast aside their livelihoods to pursue a vague, existential scientific problem, we should consider solutions that garner popular support to achieve the same objective.

Simple measures such as renewed focus on recycling, clean water, and clean air and expansions of protected areas is a positive first step toward a greater appreciation for necessary conservation. The average person will embrace taking better care of the water they drink, the air they breathe, and the awe-inspiring grandeur of nature in pristine condition. The impact of presenting complex scientific analysis that places blame without reasonable solutions only succeeds in creating a deep resentment against both the scientific community and the advocacy coalitions that support necessary actions to avoid environmental calamity. Additionally, the droning declaration of crisis after crisis will sow the seeds of intense skepticism and, in turn, will cause the American people to wholly reject any proposal that is based on a fearmongering ideological perspective. The constant insinuation of cataclysmic destruction will create counterproductive hysteria, but the introduction of simple and practical steps toward conservation will incite action. Declaring the end of the world every decade has only produced a deepening political divide, and no one on either side of the ideological debate is honestly sure of the best path toward remediation.

We must begin the work of restoring the symbiotic relationship between people and the environment if we are to secure a clean and sustainable future. If the extreme environmentalist movement's obsession with crisis politics has yielded any results, it is that the reintroduction of practical conservation would likely be a welcome reprieve from the constant threats of imminent extinction. The American people are ready and willing to walk more, use less water, reduce the use of plastics, and support gradually increasing air quality and emissions standards—but only if we can also eliminate the unrelenting, self-aggrandizing badgering from elitists who impugn our meager lifestyles while taking their private jets to the next speaking engagements. Whether it regards pristine hunting grounds, a beautiful walking trail, or a majestic national park, people from all political persuasions will support the ideas that improve our environment when we pursue substantive changes over abstract philosophies.

CHAPTER 15
Federal Budget

The federal budget is the worst form of political minutiae. The ultimate experience in watching the proverbial sausage being made is exploring the nuances of the vast expenditures of the federal government. While budgets may not be the preferred topic of conversation for the average American, the consequences of fiscal mismanagement can be the difference between prosperity and economic turmoil. Unfortunately, the federal budget has been abandoned in favor of an endless barrage of continuing resolutions to fund essential services. The deepening divide between the major political parties is causing uncertainty to impede the progress of economic development.

Passing a budget in Congress is difficult, but in recent years it has become impossible. Factions within the government have organized to advocate for the specific spending allocations that benefit them politically. Austerity has become the focus of fiscal conservatives, and over-promising is the habit of liberals. The result is a variety of unfunded mandates and campaign pledges that are impossible to fulfill without a broad agreement in Congress. Despite the advantages of passing a federal budget, no party is willing to take the political risk to reach across the aisle for the benefit of the country. Instead, each side remains firmly entrenched in its unfounded and stubborn belief that its opponents seek to destroy the fabric of our nation by abandoning our moral and economic commitments.

Beyond the constant bickering over resource allocation, the real cornerstone of our democracy is stability. A stable fiscal environment provides the foundation required for economic growth and sustained optimism among the public. The budget is not only consequential for the various departments that depend on consistent funding, but it is also a performance measure for our political leaders. No budget is going to fulfill all promises, but passing a budget indicates that Washington, DC, is functioning at a level commensurate with our expectations as voters. When spending priorities divide the nation to the point of a government shutdown, there is a severe risk that completing the necessary tasks associated with governance are becoming too politicized and overwhelming.

No matter the political party in power, there must be a consensus among our elected representatives that a comprehensive annual budget is the least they can do to provide stability for the nation. A more significant effort must be made to incorporate the priorities of both parties, thereby setting a new precedent that ideology can guide but not dictate the terms of normal operations. Each continuing resolution that provides short-term funding for the government slowly erodes our faith in the leaders we elect, and ultimately it adversely impacts our belief that the American experiment can survive the long-term battle for political power.

CHAPTER 16
On Expectations

We are accountable only to our ambition, not other people's expectations. It is when we begin to conduct a comparative analysis of our lives against others' that we start to suffer from the plague of inadequacy and adjust our goals to meet the path that is most socially acceptable. In the age of social media, the problem of groupthink and collectivism is only exacerbated and contributes to the dissipation of individual experience and achievement as a unique measure of personal expectations.

Instead of becoming exceptional at being ourselves, we become obsessed with outdueling our friends, family, and strangers at achieving accelerated mediocrity. Possessions, job titles, and vacations have supplanted contentment as our chief measure of self-worth. The results are a teetering foundation for our self-esteem and endless attempts to impress others rather than satisfy the objectives that maximize our potential. Personal accountability and consistent introspection become the relics of a bygone era when the lust for "likes" overwhelms our social consciousness. In time, every element of our lives becomes a show for followers rather than a deeply personal journey to meet our definition of success.

We will find that our current measure of achievement violates the cardinal rule for individual contentment. Joy is derived from our positive impact in the lives of people we encounter daily, and peace is the result of finding a path in life that provides contentment when no one is looking. When happiness is a private moment rather than a public reaction, we will find the feeling to be far more enjoyable and the result to be a demonstrable increase in our self-worth. It may seem that we have lost our identity in the process of gaining acceptance and notoriety, but the return of the inner dialogue as the most critical conversation is inevitable. That feeling of emptiness and dread with the direction of our lives cannot be overcome until we focus on finding a purpose that serves others and justifies our existence. As future generations learn from the mistakes of those who engage in a codependent relationship with technology, they will gain a deeper appreciation for the opportunities to experience a life that is lived instead of recorded.

CHAPTER 17
Genocide

The twenty-first century must be the time when we relegate the purposeful infliction of human suffering to the bowels of history. Genocide in all forms, and for all ill-conceived reasons, is the darkest manifestation of the corrupted soul. Too often, nations and their leaders attempt to disguise their cowardice in the pursuit of cooperation and international justice, yet there can be no justice when the innocent are swept from existence. All of our economic and social pursuits are in vain if we fail to take action on behalf of those subjected to unspeakable crimes. Unfortunately, the American pastime of righteous indignation has not grown so wild as to include the individuals in dire need of humanitarian support and immediate action. The limitations of our political will prevent us from taking concrete steps to end the daily march toward destruction millions of people suffer through beyond our borders. In the United States, political coalitions and social justice causes are limited to our narcissistic view of utopia and fail to consider the battles against barbarism that continue to rage around the globe. The rising tide of reform and equality needs to be distributed in equal measure to all peoples, not merely those within the social structure we build around our interests.

Our leaders have failed us by falling prey to the excessive whims of the privileged and seeking votes rather than justice for those who have no recourse or representation. As long as we concern ourselves with manufactured social media outrage and allow political leaders to appeal only to our narcissism, we will continue down the path of geopolitical corruption and the relinquishment of our moral authority. The United States is a leader in the causes of freedom, but that position is in jeopardy the longer we allow dictators to hold innocent people in physical and emotional imprisonment. It is also essential to keep in mind that people are not to be used as pawns in proxy confrontations between nations, and fundamental human rights are not bargaining chips to be used to gain an advantage in political or economic negotiations. Voters cannot be the only people of significance at the critical juncture when lives are at risk, and similarly, the vanity of the American electorate cannot be appeased while the deaths of millions of people are reduced to headlines. We cannot forget that squabbling over equal pay and other important gender-related issues is a luxury when millions of women and children are subjected to unknown horrors beyond our borders on a daily basis. The dark ages have yet to end for those who reside under the auspices of authoritarian brutality.

The relinquishment of our global moral imperative has only succeeded in eroding the shared values that influence domestic social behavior. We have adopted the platform of tribalism and rejected the ideals of fair consideration and kindness. Identity politics has replaced long-held notions of cooperation and a belief in the underlying principles of freedom. When we are confronted with apparent international violations of basic human rights, we prefer to retreat into the ideology of isolation, and our political leaders choose to follow suit and delegate our obligation as the defenders of freedom to corrupt and ineffective international organizations. When redlines are crossed, we have become yet another nation that lacks the courage to stand firm and steadfast in the face of evil. America should be the united nation that cedes no power to an international body that has proven to be easily corruptible and unable to address the persistent use of genocide to solidify political power. Many foreign leaders cannot see beyond their ambitions and private objectives, and they fail to care for the people who offer no value beyond the intrinsic desire to defend life.

In the wake of globalization, a new definition of a superpower is required. Humanitarian aspirations must supplant military conquest; thereby, we can lead the world into a new definition of ethical consciousness. Those who refuse to comply with the standards of international conduct should not be met with violence but rather with the power of economic persuasion as each nation becomes increasingly dependent on the prosperity of another. Even when action is not advisable, we must remain steadfast in our moral obligation to call evil by its name. The theft of innocence, freedom, and life itself are crimes that require direct admonishment and, when possible, swift intervention to alleviate. Generations have been subjected to the darkest elements of the human condition, yet the courage to speak the truth regardless of the geopolitical consequences remains the lone hindrance to the unmitigated infliction of mass destruction. While a plethora of weapons agreements have become the subjects of international cooperation and strategic alliances, the power of hate and divisiveness is still wielded by dictators and despots as the final vestiges of human omnipotence. Those who sit in chains around the globe should always know that they are not doomed to become the forgotten faces of conflict and that we are expending every resource at our disposal to counteract the diminishment of human rights.

CHAPTER 18
Gun Rights

The right to keep and bear arms is an increasingly antiquated legal right that was initially intended to provide constitutional support for state militias. An organized military structure has supplanted the time of militias, and the foundation of gun ownership has been rendered null and void beyond our cultural obsession with personal protection. Limiting gun rights may come at a steep political cost, but the inability to act legislatively continues to accrue a significant human toll. Operating without regard for the potential benefits of responsible gun ownership or the profound cultural connotations would be unwise; however, choosing to placate powerful interest groups to the detriment of public safety is an even graver concern. A balance between under-regulated ownership and the elimination of individual gun rights is possible, but no solution will be effective if the tentacles of corporate interests and the influence of campaign contributions remain higher priorities than protecting innocent life.

We must stop equivocating gun rights with an abstract perception of individual liberty. No one in the twenty-first century is going to thwart the confiscation of their freedom, if the government had the audacity to exert absolute control, with the rifle stuffed inside their closet. With modern military tactics or even police resources, it is possible to eliminate any individual who poses a threat with little fanfare. The notion that an untrained militia consisting of husbands and wives shooting at shadows from their front porch will stave off impending subjugation from a government is comical. The delusion that personal firearms will deter a government, and that the ensuing battle for liberty will be the subject of nationalistic folklore, is a perfect illustration of the inherent absurdity of widespread gun ownership in modern America.

Owning firearms for personal protection inside the home or for sporting purposes such as hunting are reasonable justifications for continuing the tradition of gun ownership. The people who believe they can effectively thwart potential danger with guns have a right to carry; however, many of the weapons currently available for purchase at sporting goods stores and gun shows extend beyond the boundary of reasonable self-defense. Furthermore, firearms used for hunting are generally limited to a small number of models compared to the entirety of the current gun market. Exceptions for common uses ingrained in specific cultural or social traditions are a reasonable compromise to achieve a comprehensive policy objective.

If owning guns for protection and hunting is to remain an integral part of our constitutional rights, there must be an accompanying effort to improve safeguards when purchasing firearms. Eliminating gun deaths is impossible, especially considering that criminals are unlikely to follow the law to obtain a weapon in the first place, but many of the heinous examples of mass shootings can be eliminated by implementing common-sense reforms. Extended waiting periods, mental health screenings for the purchasers and residents of their homes, and more extensive background checks are not foolproof measures, but they do add a layer of protection to differentiate between the law-abiding gun owner and the perpetrators of the next mass shooting. Fingerprint technology can also be used to ensure the owner of the gun is the only person who can discharge the weapon. Also, accompanying restrictions on the type of weapons available to the public will reduce the likelihood of guns capable of mass murder falling into the hands of the mentally deranged.

With each mass shooting, we become a weaker nation. The discourse over gun rights is more absurd and tribalistic than ever before, and as a result, the victims of gun violence become pawns in an ideological battle rather than the final straws that create a swell of support for a reasonable compromise. The core of the political divide is the fact that we wait until a tragedy strikes to begin the debate and discuss the possible risks of gun ownership while the names of murdered children run on the scroll at the bottom the television. Instead, we should learn from the past and begin the conversation without the emotional overtones of recent bias distorting our logic. The knowledge that another tragedy is inevitable if the current environment persists should be a sufficient motivator for political leaders to take up the issue on their own accord. Guns will always have a place in the past, present, and future of our country, but we need to modernize the interpretation of the Second Amendment to be inclusive of people who wish to bear arms without ignoring the inherent dangers of living in a weaponized society.

CHAPTER 19
On Free Markets

We are so dedicated to our aimless pursuit of change that we fail to realize that justice today is the seed of injustice tomorrow. The building blocks of equality need to be carefully arranged to avoid disrupting further construction by future generations. The insistence on cultural and social absolutes as a means to formulate a new economic path will not resolve the inconsistencies within our advocacy framework. We demand equality as if a single individual has the power to grant such a request. And we misrepresent past failures and disguise them as poor outcomes built on good intentions. When either political party, along with their supporters, implements a failed policy without acknowledging the apparent flaws, it distorts our path to an effective solution. Eventually, it will be necessary to move our discussion beyond platitudes and begin to mend the tattered remnants of social and economic cohesion.

The system of free markets, entrepreneurialism, and unrelenting ambition provide economic benefits by introducing incentives that promote hard work and educational achievement. If we turn away from the concept of free markets and instead institute a centrally controlled financial system where mandates direct economic activity, then what is our motivation to pursue excellence when the government dictates outcomes? There is no equity achieved in a system operated by the same class of people we blame for subjugating the groups who are severely impacted by the inefficient distribution of economic opportunity. Free markets provide the best chance for advancement and success, but the invisible hand is slowly appearing in the form of political elites who insist they have the prescription for equal prosperity. Instead, we will end up with an economic system that is tightly controlled to hinder the flow of money to the successful, and redistribute funds to the perceived victims of system inefficiency. No financial strategy will grant more power to the average man or woman than the free market system in which we operate, where each choice is an opportunity for personal advancement, and those in power can be held accountable without inducing the turmoil of market instability. Capitalism remains the only economic system in which each individual can decide for themselves how to best use their skills and impose a monetary value on their abilities.

Deservedness is not a function of wealth but rather an indication of talent and ambition. The response to injustice cannot be the equal distribution of poverty. Hapless attempts at Robin Hood economics will not cause the masses to become wealthy or lead to increased levels of ingenuity that are required to sustain prosperity. The result will instead be an exodus of talent to the remaining bastions of meritocracy where highly skilled labor is exchanged for monetary gain. Controlling the movement of entrepreneurs and scholars will require the erosion of freedom to forcibly remove the best and brightest from their money and titles. This is the natural progression of a society where success is impugned, and the bastardization of equality becomes the manipulative tool of opportunistic populists. Fairness cannot be achieved by plundering the prosperity of others. A free market does not equally distribute scarce resources, but it does allow individuals to determine their outcomes by providing a series of choices that lead to personal success or failure. A government offers no second chances when economic freedom is constrained; however, a free market offers as many chances as we are willing to take.

CHAPTER 20
Health Care

The stakes are too high in health care for policy development to be led by the shortsighted rantings of political demagogues. Outside of medical professionals, we all have a limited understanding of the strengths and weaknesses of the system and often suggest solutions based on our own anecdotal experiences. Crafting an effective policy that will serve our collective interests well into the future is not achieved by wielding a hammer of presuppositions that fail to depict the shortcomings we currently face. When the lives of real people hang in the balance, pursuing rapid change with ill-conceived policies will lead to a myriad of unintended consequences. Watching people suffer from a broken health-care system is a difficult circumstance, but when we discuss the available alternatives, we must have the bipartisan resolve to do more than put a Band-Aid on a generational crisis.

The identity of the American health-care system has become a convoluted assortment of directives that symbolize the ideology of each administration more than our desire for a functional and efficient approach to medicine. Furthermore, each solution brought forth by either party represents a philosophy rather than a plan of practical guidance and is therefore of little use to patients or their doctors. Pursuing a solution is a legitimate endeavor, but the needs of an entire country should be the primary consideration, and currently, the rhetoric is centered on an emotional plea in which rare examples are used to represent the norm. The first step in establishing the identity in American medical care is to appreciate that we have the medical infrastructure, technology, and capital resources to build the best health system on earth. A foundation of superior competence is a crucial resource advantage that should not be overlooked through the course of finding a solution. We do not need to model our system after countries that lack the human-capital resources or the creativity to achieve a higher level of care. If our leaders have an original thought, health-care policy is the perfect opportunity to express a new idea that might serve as the example other countries follow.

Once we recognize the assets that exist within our health-care system, we can begin to discern the underlying values that medical care in the United States should represent. The first value is a strong commitment to efficiency. Patients should not have to face long waits to access primary care, and doctors should not be so consumed with regulatory requirements that their time listening to patients is severely hampered. The doctor-patient relationship should be strengthened; therefore, implementing cumbersome bureaucratic regulations and additional administrative duties would not be wise. When doctors have the opportunity to be attentive to the needs of their patients, the result is a more efficient process of diagnoses and treatments. When each day begins, we need to ensure that doctors and other medical professionals are enthusiastically meeting their goals of helping the people who need their assistance. Our first priority should be fully supporting the role of health-care professionals by providing the resources they need to execute their duties flawlessly. Implementing a system that is simplified, transparent, and cost-effective is part of the new identity for our health-care services that will empower doctors to deliver the best care possible.

The second core value that will help us define the identity of our health-care system is affordability. Insurance companies, hospital systems, and public agencies are either oblivious or purposefully negligent of an effort to maintain reasonable prices. When a patient visits a medical office, they should know the cost of each service and be able to take ownership of their health with a transparent, symbiotic relationship between their pocketbook and the medical service provider. Delegating financial responsibility for inflated health-care costs from the patient to the taxpayer is a populist ploy and in no way represents an appropriate response to the tremendous economic burden health-care costs have become for American families. Each party invested in quality care should be compensated appropriately for their expertise, and we cannot continue using the doctor's salary as a clever diversion while we ignore the outrageous regulation-driven inefficiencies that inflate prices.

Prescription drug prices have justifiably become a focal point of the affordability discussion. There is no reason why a prescription should cost hundreds or thousands of dollars, yet when we present a discount card, it suddenly becomes affordable. Specialized treatments and rarely used medications may be one issue, but the prevalence of rising prices for essential medicines is quickly extinguishing the hope of financial stability for an untold number of American families. A trip to the pharmacy should never represent a choice between a necessary medication and buying food, yet the convoluted price structure for prescription drugs has caused many people to encounter that exact scenario. Our identity moving forward must include a market for affordable prescription drugs that alleviates the financial strain of such costs on young and old alike.

Access is another problem associated with the current health-care system that is in desperate need of an overhaul. Access is pertinent in two distinct categories. First, all people in the United States should have access to quality medical services for preventative care, maintenance care, and treatment. Modern iterations of this objective have manifested in the advent of a variety of clinics that have extended hours of operation and offer a low-cost alternative to emergency-room service at the hospital. Further supporting the development of clinics is an effective way to alleviate problems with access for essential services and provide a practical alternative to the surging insurance rates that have priced many Americans out of the market.

The second element of access is the ability to utilize the supposed benefits of health insurance entirely. The insurance system, if it is to remain intact, should be profitable but should also be significantly simplified so the insured can easily understand the inclusions and limitations of their benefits. Additionally, the ability to choose doctors who best meet the needs of the patient should take precedence over the system of restrictive networks. An individual should not have to choose between the doctor they trust and the insurance plan they can afford.

Personal responsibility must also be included in the national identity of modern health care. We cannot continue relinquishing common sense in favor of political correctness to the detriment of all people. Health-care costs are being driven to astronomical heights because insurers must account for higher-risk customers, and doctors are facing a rise in the instances of preventable conditions. There must be incentives embedded in the system that provide lower costs for the healthy, not just the young, and the autonomy for doctors and insurers to have frank conversations with patients about the individual factors that cause them to have increased insurance rates. Personal health and well-being can no longer be limited to a national dialogue about insurance-related preventative care, primarily when the essential discussion of diet and exercise have become cultural taboo.

What is ultimately needed is a simplified model of care. Medicaid for all is an attractive proposal, but for those of us who have experienced the second-rate care sometimes associated with the Medicaid and Medicare production models, we know it will turn out to be a long-term disaster that is not commensurate with our outstanding medical resources. Mediocre care for all is not a valid alternative to outstanding care for many. Maintaining quality cannot be discounted in the rush to control price. There is also a variety of pitfalls associated with the strictly capitalist model, in which the poor can be easily overlooked and suffer from a deficit of resources that help them take ownership of their medical care. As with most political issues, the solution lies somewhere in the middle of the two ideological perspectives. Moving those in poverty and individuals with preexisting conditions into a modified health-care program founded on personal and affordable care may be the best solution to ensuring that all people have access to the medical resources they need to not only survive but flourish.

The people who wish to pay for insurance to cover potential costs should also be allowed to do so. Moving high-risk individuals into the revised public program, should, in theory, lower the costs for the remaining participants in the private insurance pool. Oversight and accountability are undoubtedly key facets of adequate health care, but they should never be so cumbersome as to dictate or adversely impact the care a person wishes to receive. Mandates will prove expensive and counterproductive to the stated mission of increasing access and affordability. Meanwhile, common sense and autonomy for both patients and their doctors will create the regulatory balance necessary to produce effective results. The first step in the process is to stop pointing toward other nations for guidance and to begin outlining the health-care priorities of our people. No nation has achieved optimal performance in health services; therefore, our mandate is to act with creativity and a bipartisan mindset to develop a new approach.

CHAPTER 21
Higher Education

College was once the standard for intellectual development and a place where gifted and ambitious young people could enhance their credentials to find the best jobs available. Now a college degree is often attained with minimal effort; a student can change majors until he or she finds the easiest courses and can partake in all the debauchery that represents the esteemed university experience. The entire industry has lost its identity and is enthralled with the prospects of higher tuition, buildings that serve as monuments for egomaniacal leaders, and degree programs that attain rankings rather than jobs for their graduates. Additionally, the practice of teaching, which is the primary expectation we should have for professors, has been abandoned and delegated to graduate assistants, while the most qualified minds at the university endeavor to publish journal articles and continue their endless searches for grant funding. Great professors still exist, but they are increasingly becoming the exception rather than the norm, and they find themselves overwhelmed with responsibilities as students flock to their classrooms to discover the last remaining morsels of useful information on campus. The professor focused on teaching, caring, and leading is almost as rare as the student who takes their studies seriously. Correlation may not indicate causation, but it seems the administration, faculty, and students are failing to fulfill their obligations in equal measure.

The corporatized nature of higher education has allowed business interests to obscure our commitment to student outcomes. Colleges still rely on career earnings data versus high school graduates to justify the necessity of a degree, yet the real economic benefits to students upon graduation are waning. Millions of graduates work for an hourly wage, accept low salaries to secure health benefits, or work in positions that do not require a college degree. Instead of a degree differentiating job candidates, the plethora of college graduates in the job market causes young people to be vulnerable to manipulation and exploitation. The graduates who do find gainful employment are willing to work longer hours without accompanying salary increases because they understand that millions of underemployed job seekers are ready and willing to take their place. To reduce the likelihood of discontent, employers provide meaningless promotions in the form of titles that satisfy the ego of the social media generation and have become a form of compensation in corporate America. For now, "senior regional vice president" on an office door is a sufficient psychological device to stave off the impending rebellion of overeducated and underpaid employees. Unfortunately, the college degree has become the new participation trophy, where friends, family, and employers celebrate an accomplishment that makes a dwindling contribution to the bottom line.

Another aspect of higher education that has quickly evolved into a crisis for college students is the albatross of student-loan debt that hangs around the neck of graduates for decades after they attend their final lecture. When leaders developed the modern terminology of higher education administration, they associated a subpar education with equal access and believed suffocating student debt would serve as a suitable substitute for affordability. Rather than lower tuition and consider the financial positions of recent graduates, leaders in higher education blame stagnant federal and state grant and scholarship funding for the increasing necessity of student loans. While degree programs expand, construction projects commence, and universities crawl up the rankings ladder with blind arrogance while students watch their loan balances increase by thousands of dollars each semester. Many students are left to hope that jobs exist that will allow them to simultaneously maintain their student loan payment and move out of their parents' basements. Stewardship, ethics, and accountability have quickly become irrelevant in higher education vernacular.

While the education industry may have abandoned the traditional ideals that made it an indispensable milestone of adolescent development, the objectives of change that support the career aspirations and financial stability of students remain attainable. Colleges must first reconsider their proclivity for expansion. The surplus of universities that provide a subpar educational experience must alter their approach by offering fewer programs that provide the highest level of academic training. With fewer programs, many colleges could fully utilize the buildings on campus that already exist and concentrate their faculty and administrative efforts on a few highly rated and expertly executed degree programs that ensure students are fully qualified for employment opportunities in their chosen fields. Leaders in higher education should embrace their strengths and begin to consider eliminating the programs that struggle for both enrollment and funding.

Colleges must also come to terms with the affordability crisis. Financial habits that lead to sustained prosperity and stability should be reinforced in the university environment. Instituting a tuition rate that requires a loan balance higher than their annual salary upon graduation is a total abandonment of the fiduciary responsibility that institutions should have for their students. Colleges should consider potential austerity measures within the budget that would allow the donations and revenue they produce to increase the availability of institutional scholarships or lower the overall cost of attendance. A college degree with minimal debt will enable the industry to flourish because it will alter the prevailing notion among students who are beginning to question the wisdom of accumulating massive student debt. If colleges continue to view access to student loans as an alternative to fiscal responsibility, they will find future generations reluctant to accept their assertion that a degree is a prerequisite for success.

The final step colleges must consider to sustain their crucial role in economic and workforce development is to allow open access to freshman-year studies. If colleges shift their competitive application process to the end of freshman year, then they can accurately predict likely performance in the remaining course of study. This shift will bridge the gap between ideological perspectives by making the first year of study free to all students and the remaining years at a tuition rate that is affordable and commensurate with the quality of the educational experience. "Diversity" is a popular term, but it is only attainable when students are provided access and judged on their performance in college courses rather than their grades in high school or standardized test scores. This model provides the basis for a true meritocracy in which every student has an equal opportunity to succeed. Higher education must be affordable, impartial, and student-oriented, and it must become the symbol for academic and economic success that allows entry for all people who aspire to succeed.

CHAPTER 22

On Free Speech

Let us not be so enthralled by our private sensibilities that we insist they become law. Nothing stifles free speech more than the fear of condemnation in the public domain; therefore, our thirst for truth is replaced by an overwhelming desire for acceptance. Free speech is no longer free when it is governed by vigilante mobs and appropriated by groups who seek to silence alternative perspectives. If every ignorant utterance is considered a crime in the court of public opinion, who will be left to speak?

Another fork in the road has presented itself on our journey through history. We may choose to tolerate the speech we find reprehensible because it is rightfully spoken, or we may set forth on the ambiguous path toward censorship. We can criminalize both speech and action if we like, but it is essential that we appreciate the difference and refrain from equating one with the other. The ideas that lead to progress are born of freedom, and without the willingness to present our thoughts freely, our ability to discern right from wrong and hate from love will be irreparably damaged. Who will determine what constitutes acceptable speech in the next generation when we have no way of doing so now? There is honor in the mission to curb hate and erase our predilection for inflammatory speech, but there is no way to create a standard for conduct and guidelines for discourse that permanently alter our unique thoughts and beliefs. The best method for changing hearts and minds is to allow peace and acceptance to compete with their rivals in a free exchange of ideas.

The correct choice is always to err on the side of freedom. When a person violates the sensibilities of another, they have committed no violation at all. Our tolerance for change is growing, yet our openness to discussing the choices before us wanes, and that has the potential to create an ideological vacuum from which harmful notions are created. The destructive ideas and speech we despise are born from the exact environment we strive to create. When people are conditioned to subdue their cognitive autonomy in favor of ideological unity, they quickly surrender their unique identity in the pursuit of acceptance. In the end, we will lose our voices in the furious attempt to silence others.

CHAPTER 23

Journalism

Good journalism is the last defense we have against propaganda and the growing plague of misinformation. We may not always agree with the perspective that is espoused, but journalists have to be the keepers of truth, no matter how inconvenient the truth may be. When journalism is branded an enemy amid an ideological war, it is essential to ardently defend the practice of questioning the powerful and thwarting corruption. Those who write facts instead of opinions, and truth rather than commentary, are the defenders of liberty who are tipping the scale on the people's side of the balance of power.

In recent years, especially with the growth of digital media, journalism has begun the slow decline toward extinction. Instead of presenting facts for the reader, many choose to construct headlines for attention. Words are twisted and actions misconstrued in search of notoriety and profit, while the people are left floundering in the wake and hoping someone can lead us back to the origin of critical analysis. We cannot survive as a nation if the truth is obscured by the purveyors of news. Additionally, we have reached critical mass when scores of Americans decry the existence of a media conglomerate they view as more partisan than themselves. The short-term attraction of partisan viewership is not a wise choice when the survival of neutrality and objectivity is at stake.

The issue at hand is not that all journalists have compromised their principles in search of acceptance and applause, but rather that the mere notion of impropriety is enough to destroy the presumption of fairness members of the media once enjoyed. A single story written for the benefit of a particular ideology will irreparably damage the reputation of journalism. This is especially true when politicians seek to exploit the skepticism and fear of a nation and direct their anger back toward the stewards of free speech. The stakes have never been higher, and the standard of truth journalists must follow are beyond the platitudes of any politician or titan of industry.

To properly defend the institutions that protect us all from the metastasizing crawl of corruption and deceit, journalists must remain a neutral voice in the face of partisanship. No political enemy is worth compromising our values to vanquish. It is possible, as it has been in the past, to separate our worldview from the critical stories that are being written. We cannot falter under the tremendous strain of social and political upheaval and begin defining truth based on our presuppositions. Journalism is the art of turning facts into a concise description of our hidden reality. Remaining steadfast in the mission of justice will suffice, even as the tolerance for facts diminishes. Journalists must refrain from picking a side as the ideological fight for the future of America reaches a fever pitch. When neutral observers become political soldiers, we all lose the battle for truth.

CHAPTER 24
LGBT Rights

The rights of the LGBT community must be secured as a part of a broader effort to find an equilibrium of equality for all underrepresented groups in the United States. Discrimination and implicit bias should be eliminated through the implementation of a social structure that accepts people for who they are and values their contributions to American culture. Freedom cannot be guaranteed for anyone in this country unless it is provided to all people. While legislation is a positive first step to offer adoption rights, marriage equality, and full legal standing for same-sex couples, there is a need for a dramatic shift in the treatment of members of the LGBT community.

Equality is not measured in the eyes of the law only but rather indicates a full measure of tolerance and acceptance within both legal and social structures. What must be accomplished to secure LGBT rights is the rejection of bigotry actively concealed under the guise of cultural and religious tradition. Individuals should not be compelled to embrace the identity of another, but they should recognize that a person who is different from themselves still deserves the same level of respect and dignity. The distinctions that make us unique are the same characteristics that add tremendous value to our social and economic systems. Instead of embracing each individual for their contributions to our society, too often we prefer to engage in a destructive pattern of condemnation and judgment, or at best, ambivalence.

All people, regardless of their sexual identity, should be embraced, loved, and welcomed because they have equal value as human beings. When two consenting adults choose to share their lives, it is not the business of advocacy coalitions or religious groups to dictate the rights that will be granted or withheld. The only threat posed by the LGBT community is that we risk limiting our own freedoms in the course of intentionally excluding certain groups from fully realizing their right to equality.

The bastardization of religious philosophy is a significant barrier to cultural progress and the effort to see all people embraced for the diverse experiences they share. It is counterintuitive to consider any person who is made by God to be considered an abomination by nature of their existence as their true self. There is no defense of intentional exclusion and bodily or emotional harm provided in the Bible or any other religious document traditionally used to condemn members of the LGBT community. The use of manufactured moral authority to obscure or eliminate the freedoms of others is a direct contradiction of the foundational tenets of religious philosophy. If we choose to continue down the age-old path of using religion as a coercive device, we will only succeed in achieving the mutually assured destruction of the rights we all seek to fully realize in the pursuit of life, liberty, and happiness. If the United States truly stands on moral principles, then we must recognize that our directive is to treat all people with equal measures of kindness and respect. Our highest objective should be to enshrine equal rights in the legislative and constitutional expression of our tolerance and appreciation for all people.

CHAPTER 25
On Justice

The legal system is not broken, but we must demand a higher standard of conduct from critical stakeholders. Each day justice is served without controversy or complaints. Dangerous people are removed from society, and in a vast majority of cases, innocent defendants are found not guilty. The issue that we face is not an unjust system where innocence is a secondary notion, but rather that guilt can result in unbalanced sentencing and manipulative tactics are used to maximize punishment rather than achieve rehabilitation.

The very foundation of stability in the modern world is an efficient and fair legal system where grievances are remedied and the innocent are protected from those who seek to violate their inalienable rights. The United States has succeeded in creating a method to determine guilt and innocence, but it is not without the problems associated with a complex criminal justice apparatus. The inappropriate distribution of influence has obscured the divide between justice and inequality. Prosecutorial autonomy, paired with rigid and discriminatory sentencing, has caused members of our communities to fear a system that should represent the protection of their rights. The evasion of justice by the privileged may be a statistical overstatement, but it remains a pervasive notion among the people who know they could not afford the defense necessary to maintain their freedom. Justice is not blind when an innocent person accepts a plea deal because they lack the resources to fight or the knowledge of their rights. It is a bastardization of our legal system to permit the exploitative power of information asymmetry and continually give those in poverty a choice between degrees of guilt.

A paradigm shift is necessary to change the legal framework from an adversarial position to an advocacy role. Every person who enters the criminal justice system should be treated as innocent until proven otherwise in an evenhanded pursuit of the truth. We cannot allow emotions, public pressure, and politics to influence the process. We must reject the unethical reliance on plea bargaining to reduce the number of cases on the docket quickly. Yes, the system moves slower than we would like, but an overloaded docket is a policy problem, not the fault of an individual who must now choose between facing inflated charges or losing their right to a fair trial. We might want to consider reducing caseloads by removing the criminality or mandatory sentencing for lower-level offenses.

Even the death penalty is not immune to the manipulation that has slowly taken hold of our justice system. The death penalty can be an essential tool to permanently remove from society the perpetrators of the most heinous crimes, but too often it is used as a bargaining chip rather than a severe penalty reserved for the monsters among us. Capital punishment deserves the reverence of death and should never be allowed in cases that do not meet the most stringent criteria.

Everyday justice is served throughout this country, but that is not enough for the people who live in fear of becoming victims of the system constructed to protect their liberty. There is too little support for those in difficult circumstances, and there is little appreciation for the assumption of innocence when we begin to pursue efficiency over fairness. We continue to purposely evade true equality within the criminal justice system, both in terms of class and race. The framework for a transparent and equitable system already exists, but it is incumbent upon us to advocate for further action to alleviate the remaining problems that cause us to doubt that the equal distribution of justice is possible.

CHAPTER 26
Mental Health

The richness of the human experience has been reduced to the repetition of monotonous tasks. Middle managers determine our economic mobility, and the numbers of likes and followers determines our intrinsic value. We have relinquished control of self-esteem and happiness to faceless strangers with whom we have no tangible relationship. The inspiration of a kind word or a unique moment in time with family has dissolved into a journey to the darkest reaches of impersonal communication. The moments that were once seared into our memories as experiences that were uniquely ours are now compulsively recorded and shared with people who have no vested interest. Life is increasingly meaningless, and our daily addictions cause us to squander the morsels of value that remain.

The prevalence of depression, anxiety, and a variety of other mental health issues has become an impediment to personal growth on a national scale. Treatment is an essential aspect of addressing the overall problem, but a pill cannot be the only solution when we relinquish our humanity. Because individual value is now synonymous with social media profiles, we have become a generation of narcissists whose good deeds cannot even be discreetly executed. The only thing that remains hidden is the pervasive pain that we mask with a smile in a picture because at least for a moment, we can create the ideal conditions we struggle to find.

The alternative to a fraudulent existence where we outsource our identity is to build a foundation of service, attentiveness, and communication with the people who positively influence our lives. If we must relinquish our sense of self, let us do so in service to others, not in fruitless attempts to satisfy our vanity. We are all in need of a kind word and the comfort of human interaction, but we miss such opportunities when our attention is fixated on a screen. Let us dedicate our lives to helping those in need, rejecting the prevailing wisdom that dictates how we currently spend our time, and actively engage with our communities to create a sense of purpose within ourselves. To help where we can, no matter how small the act, is the escape from the mental anguish we experience.

We must have a reckoning with ourselves and recognize that mental health is a priority for all and not the disease of the depraved or weak. We may be able to convince ourselves that we exude the qualities of happiness and normalcy, but every individual faces moments in which they question the meaning of life or the value they bring to both their existence and the lives of others. To continue placing the burden of exclusion and judgment on those brave enough to emerge with their own difficulties is counterproductive to the core objective of effectively treating the problem. The national conversation must shift from an indictment of others to a frank discussion of the issues that affect all of us.

Developing treatments and gaining better insight as to the underlying causes of poor mental health must be a simultaneous pursuit. Part of the answer is related to medical research and discovery, and another part is addressing the social evolution that distorts our sense of self. When we consider the finality of death, at least in the scope of our existence in the current form, a lasting legacy emerges as the remedy for a temporary presence. Unfortunately, a lasting legacy is no longer defined by our impact on loved ones, but rather our occupational and digital productivity. We have convinced ourselves that social media posts are the permanent record of our existence and the only meaningful pieces of ourselves we can contribute to society. What we fail to realize is that when all people strive for permanence online, the actual result is a complete dilution of our physical impact. Recording a moment will never compare to the brilliant satisfaction of allowing ourselves to be present for the people who will learn the value of life from the example we choose to set. The lasting legacy of an individual life is not the fleeting achievement of supposed fame, but rather the positive influences we have on our children, family, and friends when we challenge ourselves to ignore the vast array of distractions and choose to be present.

CHAPTER 27
Military

When all diplomatic efforts have been exhausted, utilizing the full force of the American military must be employed to protect both our freedom at home and the sovereignty of strategic partners abroad. Maintaining our position as the leading superpower requires restraint when possible but also total dedication to victory when diplomacy proves to be a futile endeavor. The last few decades have left us pondering whether military decisions are guided by wisdom or whether they are costly results of devious political calculations. Leaders with a propensity to bloviate and present exaggerated assessments of risk have left millions of Americans—and opposing political leaders—skeptical as to the true extent of a given threat. The decision to place soldiers in peril is not a trivial concern for the military families who risk losing loved ones at the whim of a president, and taking such action should only be considered when a grave or direct threat exists.

Another result of the convoluted management of the past global crises is a crippling fear of total engagement. If we can eventually trust our government to be discerning over the use of force, then we should also understand the necessity of allowing soldiers to complete their missions without the implementation of onerous restrictions on engagement. We are continuing down the path of enabling hamstrung military personnel to make the ultimate sacrifice unnecessarily, which will only succeed in further eroding morale and diminishing the perception of the commitment we have to our defense abroad. Strategic partners will fear we lack the courage to defend common objectives, and our enemies will monopolize on our hesitation. The protection of freedom and human life around the globe ought to inspire a demonstration of non-nuclear force that causes nations observing our military might to cower in fear and permanently reconsider any future challenge of American sovereignty or power.

A key aspect of increasing the strength of our military is to ensure appropriate compensation for all personnel. The American people cannot withhold their financial support for soldiers until they have been injured or killed in action. We must take proactive steps to increase pay for members of the armed forces and make sure that veterans are not awarded with menial benefits and substandard health care after they risk their lives in defense of our freedom. Capitalism relies on assessments of value in the marketplace to assign a dollar amount to a job, but rarely do we accurately assess the monetary value of those who ensure our financial stability is protected. Every economic transaction we make relies on the assurance of security and mitigation of risk. Therefore, the people who directly provide an environment for economic growth should be rewarded with financial incentives that represent their value. Today, soldiers in a variety of roles are woefully underpaid, and a proper remedy is required if we are genuinely dedicated to recruiting the best candidates and maintaining a strong military.

The introduction of a small tax on all working Americans dedicated to military compensation would allow all of us to contribute a minute amount that will adequately reward members of the armed forces during their enlistment and beyond. The tax would be used solely for increased pay above the current monthly stipend, would incentivize enlistments, and would ensure all active duty personnel and veterans would be able to support their families in perpetuity for dutifully serving their country. A significant increase in compensation is necessary for an occupation that requires complete dedication to defending our freedom and securing the foundation of economic activity and future prosperity.

Because the safety of every citizen is potentially put at risk, debates over military funding should be excluded from the destructive political disputes that threaten to undercut our national security. The future of the country depends on financial support for technological development, weaponry innovation, and recruitment. Additionally, when the unfortunate moment arrives that military force is required, we must allow the best military minds to formulate effective strategies and create rules of engagement that follow international protocols while allowing soldiers to do the jobs for which they are trained. Our military is the most formidable force on earth, but years of mismanagement and weak political leadership have allowed inferior forces to erode the perception of our strength. Our imperative as the beacon of liberty is to ensure that the armed forces have the resources necessary to protect the innocent, stand against tyranny, and mobilize in a way that terrifies any nation or group of people who have the audacity to threaten our freedom.

CHAPTER 28
On Moral Relativism

Morality is not relative, but it does expand outside the bounds of conventional religiosity. The characteristics and principles traditionally defined as moral are not confined to a single religion and have little to do with the unique expression of faith practiced by a variety of ideologies. Each religion, in some form, has complicated and obscured the morality expressed by all people. Modern definitions of morality have served to divide and define each group within a generation. Unfortunately for the zealots who profit from the threat of damnation, the underlying aspects of morality are a unifying force when expressed in their purest form.

A simple set of objectives should serve as indicators of ethical thought and moral action. Kindness, tolerance, and respect for life are the values that unite honest people before the formal elements of specific religious behavior are introduced. While many people remain steadfast in their belief that dogmatic inadequacy will doom their brethren, it is essential to understand that those with ulterior motives use the practice of exclusion and condemnation to manipulate ordinary people. The judgment of one individual against another is a divisive practice used to limit critical thinking and rein in the limitless potential of human understanding. The aspects of life, nature, and science we do not know should be a welcome addition to our collective consciousness and do not pose a threat to the religious principles of peace and understanding. New information, social and cultural progress, and a heightened understanding of the people who define change for the future are the bricks on which the foundation of human development and achievement is built. Embracing the unknown should not be considered an adversary of an individual or collective morality but rather the benefit of exploring the outer reaches of the human mind.

Morality, as with politics, is a stronger force for productive social development and specific adherence when built upon a responsible foundation. Morality does not begin with the teachings of a church but rather the conversations within a home. Eradicating racism and bigotry requires communication centered on the principles of kindness and acceptance and ends with a new generation of Americans with no experience of past sins, and no basis for making judgments of people because of their race, nationality, gender, religion, or sexual identity. As positive social change flows upward from home, it is possible to create a government that is responsive to the sentiments of the majority without neglecting the inherent equality of the minority.

Moral relativism is the retort of the offended and not the reality of our current social and cultural conditions. We are righteous because we care for our families, our communities, and our inherent right to be free. Taking steps to protect our critical interests is not an offense to the God from which those values are derived. Americans must exercise and strengthen their ability to think critically and clearly in the face of opposition and groupthink because accountability is not a passive pursuit but rather an active engagement in productive discussion between the people and their leaders.

CHAPTER 29
Minimum Wage

The minimum wage should be commensurate with the level of experience and skill a person offers to a business. Basing minimum-wage policy on the fluctuating definition of a living wage is an illogical pursuit, considering the effect of regional inflation that can cause a living wage in one part of the country to equal abject poverty in another. Instead of making promises that garner votes rather than spur economic growth, we should implement policies that take a nuanced approach to wages and have a stronger sense of responsibility for the interests of businesses and the employees they hire.

A minimum wage should be a standard rate of pay that increases incrementally according to age and experience. A significant increase in the minimum wage should include tax incentives for employers to offset the additional cost of labor. The goal of wage increases is to improve the lives of working-class Americans and attempt to reconcile the deep divide between employees and employers, but it is shortsighted to be dismissive of the potential economic consequences. The first step is to consider that the minimum wage is intended to create a pay floor for entry-level positions. Traditionally, entry-level candidates have little to no experience and do not add sufficient value to the productivity of the business to justify a higher rate of pay. While the justification may be valid in theory, in practice, the minimum wage creates a vacuum of poverty for people with few alternatives in a take-it-or-leave-it hiring scenario.

Corporations use their leverage to exploit the financial desperation of those in poverty and are satisfied to maintain the same pay rates in perpetuity without appropriate oversight. Alternatively, people in favor of the immediate implementation of a living wage are either naive or purposely ignoring the effect such a policy would have on teenage and high school graduate employment, and the cost of goods as the fixed labor cost suddenly increases. A significant increase would also shift the burden of duties required for a traditional minimum-wage employee onto fewer workers as companies attempt to streamline their workforce to avoid paying additional people at a rate that provides diminishing returns on their labor investment. The result of poor planning on wage policy, and merely relying on platitudes to secure popular support, is a diminished quality of life for both the employees who did receive the new minimum wage and those who lose their opportunity to work at a company that is now reconsidering plans for growth.

A valuable alternative would be a proposal that accounts for the needs of all stakeholders. A minimum wage that increases with age would allow adults who are working in entry-level positions to earn suitable paychecks, while teenagers continue to have the opportunity to learn the value of hard work and responsibility without becoming a financial liability to their employers. Employees between the age of fifteen and seventeen should have a minimum wage of $8 per hour; employees between the age of eighteen and twenty should have a minimum wage of $12 per hour; and employees aged twenty-one and older should earn a minimum wage of $16 per hour.

Additionally, employers who hire new employees at $16 per hour should be exempt from payroll taxes. Businesses must have relief when they take on the social causes of politicians, and such an incentive would allow employers to hire the people they need without suffering the combined cost of additional wages and tax liabilities. The government would receive less tax revenue from employment growth, but they would also have fewer expenditures as the number of Americans requiring federal assistance shrinks. We should not be so ignorant to suppose that the business community is the model of greed, while the government is the purveyor of efficiency and virtue.

Securing appropriate wages for American workers that alleviate the incidence of poverty among the working class is an essential objective if we are to begin actively seeking to reduce inequality. Too many workers are asked to sacrifice forty hours or more of their lives each week, only to be left at a deficit in their banks account time and again. The answer to the problem is multifaceted, and wages are only one aspect of necessary change, but increased pay for millions of Americans would bring needed relief in the short term while leaders in business and government seek a broader solution. Although the problem of poverty and exploitative wages require a serious response, we must remain measured in our approach and not seek political ends with reckless abandon at the expense of sustainable economic growth. A new minimum wage will provide tangible benefits to the workers who have no leverage to advocate on their behalf. An incremental increase in pay with strategic incentives will ensure that we do not abandon the fundamental principle that wage is a representation of productive value and not an arbitrary indicator of individual deservedness.

CHAPTER 30
Police

The police departments in the United States are comprised of men and women who are dedicated to protecting their communities and ensuring that we can enjoy a peaceful existence without being subjected to potential dangers that lurk around the corner. They accept a tremendous responsibility while being paid what many of us would consider a substandard wage, especially considering the potentially deadly consequences that are inherent in their occupation. Despite being targets for ridicule and violence, a vast majority of officers maintain a disposition of restraint and kindness toward the people they protect, even when our propensity for misplaced rage turns police officers into national pariahs.

We do not fully appreciate the pressure that accompanies each encounter with an unknown person who can quickly become a fatal obstacle between the officer and their desire to return home to their spouse and children at the end of each shift. The perception that our police officers have become a marauding band of lawless executioners is a characterization guided by preconceived notions and anecdotal experiences from both the past and present. Before we fall prey to groupthink or begin to make unfounded assumptions, we should first make an effort to introduce members of the community to the officers who are working to maintain a safe and productive society. The best way to dispel harmful and bigoted notions, as has been the case in the past, is to create a constructive dialogue in which the fears and concerns that directly impact the people and the police can be fully explored. By the time a discussion descends into conflict, the opportunity for active and straightforward engagement in individual communities has been lost. When we refuse to employ reason in the moments of great turmoil, we will only succeed in reinforcing the negative and destructive stereotypes that engender ignorance.

While a majority of police officers are dedicated to community service, protecting our inalienable rights, and maintaining the law, there are far too many instances of officers who abuse their power to the detriment of innocent people. From the utilization of checkpoints in immigrant neighborhoods to the dubious traffic stops that amount to blatant harassment, wherever individual officers decide to abuse their power, they should be held accountable and punished to the full extent of the law. The standard of conduct for police officers is higher than any other public official because the gun on their belt is a coercive force that leaves the innocent targets of their aggression completely helpless to defend themselves. The blue shield of silence needs to be destroyed by the full exercise of accountability to ensure rogue officers who use their authority to fracture the community are eradicated from the force before their misdeeds have deadly consequences.

The police, along with the general public, must also reacquaint themselves with the fundamental notion that all people are innocent until proven guilty. In the age of social media, uninformed observers determining guilt in the court of public opinion have become a detriment to justice and a corrupting influence on the practice of due process. Too often, police treat people as though they have been convicted before a single piece of evidence has been presented in a court of law. It may be frustrating when the wheels of justice turn slowly, and it may violate our core sensibilities when someone who is believed to be guilty is not convicted, but there is no system more essential to maintaining peace and order than the justice system. No matter our opinion, we cannot will an innocent man to guilt, and the police must exercise even greater restraint when the consequences of a single investigative oversight can become a life sentence.

In addition to greater communication, accountability, and appreciation for presumed innocence, we must also consider common-sense measures that may save the lives of both the public and the police. Continuing to ensure every officer is equipped with a body camera and has access to ongoing mental health resources are critical in a job that can become overwhelming in an instant. Police officers are expected to execute a variety of duties seamlessly, yet we rarely consider how the substantial pressure of the job may lead to combustible interactions with members of the public. Police officers need appropriate resources to make sure they can do their jobs to the best of their abilities for the benefit of each community they serve. There are many instances in which we can become frustrated or outraged, but we need to remember that when we fear for our lives, they are the people we depend on to keep us safe. We all deserve a constructive dialogue in which each stakeholder has the opportunity to advocate for the modifications they believe would strengthen the commitment to community policing.

CHAPTER 31

On Patriotism

Despite the recent efforts to conflate tradition and populism with patriotism, there is no correlation between the sentiments. Patriotism is a unique emotion and is expressed through an attitude of appreciation. Many of us who are patriotic do not represent a religion or a political perspective, nor do we associate our love of country with a bastardized belief in supremacy or justified subjugation. The history of the United States is full of the trials and errors that naturally occur through the course of developing a new nation, but the harmful elements of our growth as a nation pale in comparison to the benefits we all have experienced. We are still recovering from the evils of slavery and grappling with persistence of racial bias, but the continual perpetuation of tolerance and appreciation for diversity will eventually cause hate to succumb to progress.

Patriotism is a simple philosophy that has been manipulated to suit the needs of people who seek to shroud their ignorance in the flag. Patriotism is not exclusive to a race, religion, or region. Instead, it is the belief that a political experiment founded on the principles of equality and liberty has transformed the world into a place where tyranny is the exception and being exceptional is the norm. The definition of an American patriot requires a modification that allows those of us with positive intent to reclaim the true meaning of pride.

We are proud of this country because we have the freedom to make mistakes and the flexibility to change course. We are proud of this country because millions of people from a variety of places can coexist free of the violence that plagues much of the world. We are proud of this country because advocacy can still spur sustainable change for those who have been mistreated in the past. We are also proud of this country because risk runs through our veins, love through our hearts, and understanding through our minds. This country is great because we can all bare our teeth at each other to solve social and political qualms, yet we know the ground beneath our feet is stable and unmoved by our political intemperance. This country can withstand simultaneous attacks on all of the founding institutions and principles, and still, the flag flies each morning as if it is unshaken by of our rhetoric. The most distinctive aspect of our country is that we can throw stones at the windows and they will not break, shake the ground and the foundation will not falter, and unleash a fire of fury, but it will not burn.

Yes, patriotism is often the prelude to a racist remark or a harmful action, but the true meaning will remain unchanged. While the masses roam the internet in search of their pound of flesh, the country continues to operate, no matter who is at the helm. We should embrace the power of patriotism to make us grateful, provide perspective, and allow us to imagine a future even brighter than the past. Generations before us purposefully excluded deserving people from the fruits of our collective labor, but that was not the fault of liberty. Instead, such exclusions were made by flawed men who believed their power of manipulation was more potent than the inertia of change. Because this country is excellent, they were eventually proven to be wrong by the very people they sought to silence. We must embrace the concept of patriotism, not for the meaning a few bigots want us to adopt, but because this country is so great that we can survive the flaws within ourselves until we realize the errors of our ways. Once we accept our shortcomings, we are equipped with all of the skills and resources to correct our mistakes. No other country can experience success and failure in equal measure and remain optimistic, productive, and utterly prepared to lead the world into a prosperous future. America is great because of the millions of unique people who fight in their own way to make us better.

CHAPTER 32

Privacy

There can be no reasonable expectation of privacy when we engage in a daily habit of selling our anonymity in the pursuit of online notoriety. We can easily prevent companies from profiting and manipulating behavior from the data they accumulate, but they continue to have unobstructed access to every aspect of our daily lives. If we wish to retain control of sensitive information, the best course of action is to exercise some semblance of self-control and refuse to engage with various platforms that we know collect our data and use it as a source of revenue. Technology companies can only be trusted to pursue ends that benefit the sustainability of their business model. Any other assumption about their intentions with our personal data is incredibly naive and misguided.

To combat the misuse of our personal information, we must stop assuming our privacy is the cost of innovation. Convenience improves the efficiency of our busy lives, but the bombardment of targeted advertisement and the potential risk to our identity and financial security negate the positive effect of the modern connectivity technology provides. Additionally, we fail to understand the extent to which our information can be used. Some applications are undoubtedly useful and further improve the human experience, but far more often, our private information is shared without regard for the potential effects on our security.

A complete rejection of modern conveniences and social media platforms is not necessary, but greater awareness of where our private information travels is an important step to regain control of our right to privacy. The government should be intervening to protect our best interests as consumers, but so far, they have fallen short of that most basic expectation. The political environment also evolves too quickly for us to assume a policy solution will save us from ourselves. Instead, while technology companies operate with reckless abandon and exploit their customers, we should become our most effective advocates and refrain from providing data that will be sold and used to either profit from our gullibility or monopolize on our ignorance. No technological innovation improves our lives to the extent that ceding our identity becomes a reasonable price.

CHAPTER 33
Public Education

The education system in the United States is in disrepair. The current functionality exemplifies the inefficiency and inadequacy associated with a plethora of programs managed by federal and state governments. Students in many school districts across the nation suffer from the policy whims of ideological instability and a complete lack of cohesion in the delivery of a practical approach to teaching. Trends in education have left our teachers with a mountain of paperwork and other bureaucratic responsibilities and no specific leadership or foundational principles to guide their instruction. When a system becomes disjointed and consistently underperforms, it is wise to consider starting anew with a proposal that is harmonious with our values as a nation and the long-term economic needs of the private sector.

The first change that needs to be adopted is a restructuring of the daily schedule for public-school students. Elementary school children standing at bus stops before the crack of dawn is the antithesis of effective time management and fails to consider the scientific importance of a corresponding relationship between the child's sleep patterns and academic performance. Additionally, the current school schedule fails to properly align with the work schedules of parents who would prefer to reduce the prevalence of latchkey kids who spend their afternoon each day with little to no supervision or direction. A simple movement of the school day back one hour will allow students the opportunity to gain additional time to sleep, thereby providing the proper conditions for effective cognitive development. The movement of one hour will also reduce the amount of time students spend outside of school before their parents arrive home from work. Aligning the schedules of students and parents will provide a better environment for positive family development and allow young students the opportunity to mentally and physically recover from each day before beginning the next.

The public-school curriculum has suffered dramatically from educational trends and policy directives. Instead of embracing the unique critical-thinking abilities that have allowed Americans to lead the world in ingenuity and entrepreneurship, we have decided to transform the classroom into a strictly convergent model that mimics other nations that do not share our cultural appreciation for creativity and divergent thinking. The result is the creation of a national identity crisis in which students have a limited vision for their potential, and educators have to choose between teaching to the test versus teaching for success.

Increasing the number of students pursuing careers in science and technology is essential, considering the global trend of economic development and the deficit of trained practitioners within STEM fields. While the incorporation of such programs is a valuable educational tool, it should not come at the expense of robust opportunities within the arts and humanities. The artistic and scientific paths of public education do not have to be mutually exclusive if the funds allotted to states and individual school districts are used efficiently. The value of divergent thinking in any field of study must become a priority to restore the curiosity and engagement of students in and out of the classroom. The droning beat of instruction and regurgitation is quickly draining the last vestige of enthusiasm from the American public-school student.

Students in the United States should not be compared to those of any other nation, and our curriculum should hold steadfast to our desire to incorporate a holistic vision for student learning. Public schools should have exceptional programs in math and science, along with a commitment to ensuring music, arts, and the humanities are equally appreciated and sufficiently funded. Our collective creativity is eroding with the elimination of fine arts programs across the country, and in a nation that decries the global proclivity for uniformity, supporting the diversity of students' interests should be our highest objective.

Support for programs that expand critical-thinking skills will also serve our long-term economic interests. The rate of global innovation and technological development indicates that the competency in highest demand for the future will be adaptability. A specific curriculum today may very well be rendered useless in a decade; therefore, it is incumbent upon leaders in education to prepare students for an environment of rapid change. The current dependence on information stability will leave students in the United States lagging instead of leading in the effort to innovate the future.

We must also endeavor to provide an environment where every child can experience the positive reinforcement that allows them to explore their unique gifts and abilities. A greater variety of extracurricular activities should be expanded and incorporated into the daily curriculum to better establish positive social relationships, a sense of identity, and higher self-esteem. Additional clubs, organizations, and athletic participation will become an integral part of the schedule and allow students to socialize and engage in activities that appeal to their specific abilities and interests. Facilitating student engagement outside the classroom will help to reduce the feeling of isolation and hopeless-ness that plagues children and adolescents who lack the positive rela-tionships with peers that build the foundation of long-term self-esteem and cognitive development.

In addition to examining the effectiveness of instruction, all stake-holders must begin to critically analyze the outcomes associated with each dollar spent on education. As the United States has increased funding for the public-school system, it has not created the intended results. Many school districts continue to face annual deficits and lack the critical tools required for proper instruction and maintenance of student enrichment activities. Too much money is allocated to the ed-ucation system for teachers to be spending their own money to make sure they have the supplies they need to execute their duties. Teachers should receive pay increases to recruit the most qualified practitioners, and they should not be burdened with the responsibility of adequately supplying their classrooms. The budget should incorporate stipends for economically disadvantaged students to receive the supplies they need to succeed academically. Of the many problems facing our pub-lic-school system, the resource deficit within each classroom is the most disgraceful sign of waste and inefficiency. States could also consider im-plementing a small tax increase to reduce the disparity of resources and funding between school districts. Having the funds to succeed should not be determined by property values when we have made a solemn vow to provide quality education to every child.

The future of our children, and the position of the United States as the leader in innovation and development, hinges on our ability to cre-ate an environment for transformational instruction. The era of severe bureaucratic impediments and inherently biased standardized testing, and the erosion of idealism and creativity, should be replaced with a system that challenges and engages students and provides teachers the autonomy to adapt their instruction to the specific needs of each class. When teachers are supported and empowered, and students are actively engaged in the learning process, our school system can begin the critical work of educating and training the next generation of Americans. Only then can students regain the freedom to pursue careers that maximize their unique gifts and potential instead of limiting their prospects to choices between cogs in the industrial machine.

CHAPTER 34

On Personal Conduct

Civility is the highest objective of the political organization and should be the commonly held ideal of anyone who yearns for the peaceful maintenance of decent society. To overcome our divisive biases, we must maintain a full appreciation for the productive qualities of restraint and mutual respect. Instead, we have rejected our common sense and sought an abstract notion of ideological adherence. Political opponents have suddenly become enemies and therefore are deserving of the full barrage of vitriol produced by advocacy mobs. Conviction and passion may be the heart of the body politic, but the intellectual conscience demanding civil discourse is the political brain deciphering true conviction from indignant ignorance.

Our own social and political identity has been corrupted by empty threats, manipulative moralizing, and unsubstantiated accusations of existential harm in the attempt to solidify partisan influence over the American electorate. We have become game pieces in a factional power struggle rather than the determinants of our own will. The most powerful tool we have is to actively resist the onslaught of political leaders who attempt to appropriate our successes and failures for their benefit. To succeed in this endeavor, we must reject the antagonistic subjugation by the political class and not allow strangers to dictate how we treat members of our community. While patience and perspective are difficult to conjure when a dystopian picture of humanity becomes the prevailing wisdom, it is essential to rely on the reality of our daily interactions to shape our perspective. The inundation of negative information cannot quell the hope we have for our own lives and the belief that our children can learn from our mistakes and work toward a more civilized future.

Respect and humility are virtues that should be exemplified by our leaders and exercised by all who seek to build a cooperative future. The path of division and conflict has been pursued to its furthest extent, and it fails to meet the needs of an educated and informed citizenry. Compromise should emerge from the bowels of naive idealism and be extolled as a device for legitimate political progress. In the United States, there are no enemies within the political discourse, only rivals pursuing the common objectives of prosperity, equality, and opportunity. With that in mind, we can no longer accept the standard retort of demonization to discredit opponents who represent nothing more than an alternative viewpoint. If we genuinely abide by the constitutional right to free speech and expression, then we should welcome the thoughts and perspectives that provide a deeper understanding of the issues that prevent positive societal development. Hate should be met with patience and ignorance with knowledge. To heal the divisions obstructing the path to shared prosperity, it is incumbent upon us that we redirect our frustration to the problem rather than the person. Ideological uniformity is not the solution; instead, we should seek a renewed appreciation for the diverse perspectives that challenge our values and cause us to ponder ideas we had yet to consider.

CHAPTER 35

Racism

The normalization of racial intolerance will never be eliminated from the bowels of fringe ideology. The practice of hate and discrimination is a purposeful aversion to critical thinking and cultural enlightenment. Those who continue to espouse an agenda of ignorance are within their constitutional rights, but they will only be pushed further into social isolation as new generations become increasingly accepting of the unique characteristics that make this country great. Instead of legitimizing hate speech through public admonishment, we would be better served to move past the rantings of white supremacists and other purveyors of hate as they preach to their dwindling choir.

A better investment of our efforts to create a more equitable environment for all people would be to begin analyzing key areas where latent racism continues to limit the opportunities for traditionally underrepresented groups. For instance, while we are all distracted by an irrelevant hate march in a city we have never visited, the best colleges continue to be plagued by single-digit African American enrollment. While we talk about a statue, Hispanic Americans and African Americans continue to be harassed by the police. While we yell about the meaning of a flag that flies in southern trailer parks, men and women from underrepresented groups fight for equal pay, equal opportunity, and a comparable level of respect in the corporate workforce. Today's real oppressors display friendly smiles, hold signs of solidarity, and make grand declarations of change while they work to impede the march of progress.

Continuing to be aware of the many avenues by which we can reduce the effect of racism is important, but we also need to take a moment to examine the macrosocial conditions in the country. Diversity is no longer a novelty in American culture, and great efforts have been made to ensure children understand that diversity and appreciation of all people will provide the greatest benefit to society and enrichment in their own lives. The answer may not be the short-term solution we all strive for, but the propensity for intolerance will diminish with each generation raised in a home where respect is associated with conversations about race, gender, ethnicity, religion, and sexual orientation. Only over time, with proper instruction in the house and in the foundational institutions that support childhood growth and development, will the hope of equal opportunity for all finally come to fruition.

The bridge between the world as it exists and the future we wish to create will be built by extolling the virtues that heal the racial divide. Teaching victimhood is equally as destructive as ethnic supremacy when the result is a warped perception of human value and potential, either in oneself or others. The constant insistence that every negative interaction between two people is a result of latent prejudice is more harmful than constructive. The people who have built empires on the anguish of the oppressed can only maintain their power by keeping their ideology relevant. Their objective is accomplished by crushing the spirit of individuality and controlling the national dialogue. The purveyors of racial injustice and provocateurs of manufactured oppression fail to acknowledge the improving reality that threatens to supplant their legacy in the modern equal rights movement.

Instead of depending on a series of filters to formulate our perspective, we need to examine the reality of our own lives instead. Racial discrimination exists in our society, but so do tolerance, understanding, and respect in increasing volume. The people who deny the existence of racism in any capacity are admonished, yet those who insist racism remains the very foundation of our society are promoted, apparently, without an appreciation for the negative consequences; both messages produce in equal measure. If we are to move forward peacefully and constructively, it will be necessary for all advocates to take ownership of their unique experiences and stop leaning on platitudes to create ideological momentum.

CHAPTER 36
Separation of Church and State

Personal and public morality have been combined into a complex concoction that distorts the clear delineation between the two. The separation of church and state provides a clear boundary between the two concepts of moral understanding, but the point where they overlap is where the confusion occurs. Religion and social cohesion can be complementary facets of moral development, but neither belongs in the domain of a single entity. When we lose sight of the value of separation, the result is a conflict derived from the fear that one may negate the impartiality of the other. However, when we consider both elements independently of the other, we see the inherent benefit of both church and state working exclusively and simultaneously to strengthen our bond.

Public morality is comprised of the principles that govern our behavior, regardless of religious ideology. Secular laws are the foundation of the public morality, and we all obey their tenets out of respect for our freedom and the right of our fellow human beings to live without fear that their safety, security, or property may be compromised without recourse. The original intent of public morality may have been derived from certain religious principles, but they have been followed for their secular practicality. We have entered into a collective agreement that public morality serves the needs of the majority and secures an environment suitable for the development of economic productivity, which improves the lives of all people. For it is trade, not tradition, that provides the thread in which we are all woven into the social, cultural, and economic fabric of America.

Personal morality is comprised of the teachings that are specific to a single religion. Such lessons have no place in the operations of the state beyond their influence on universal laws we have carried from the religious realm to the secular. There is good reason personal morality is not permitted to interfere with the duties of governance or education because it is far too subjective to regulate or predict. Personal morality always has been and will remain best suited for instruction within the home. It is not the job of teachers to relay religious principles to our children, and it is not the job of our representatives to act as saints rather than senators. The separation of church and state is not intended to minimize the importance of religion but instead to make sure religious principles remain firmly entrenched in the domain of personal morality. Too much time and attention are required to satisfy the people of this nation for us to seek to please their gods as well.

CHAPTER 37
On Politics

The political class has been placed on a pedestal that creates the illusion they are superior in character and knowledge. Instead of setting reasonable expectations for their proficiency in governance, we prefer to construct caricatures that limit their ability to function as ordinary people. Meanwhile, the new sport of candidate destruction allows us to dictate absurd parameters and then express our disappointment when no man or woman meets our outlandish standards. To create a more functional model of governance, we must stop assuming that political candidates possess skills far beyond our own. If we understand they are ordinary people seeking to serve their country in public office, it will provide an opportunity for shared respect and productivity. We all fail our democracy when we tear down its leaders merely to prove they do not fit the image we have imposed.

It is essential to hold politicians accountable for their actions in their private lives and their roles as public servants, but we cannot lose sight of their humanity. Flaws and missteps are an inevitable occurrence. We should strive to be better, but ultimately, the goal should be to encourage good men and women to seek elected office without fear that their lives can be destroyed in the process. When the level of scrutiny reaches the point of absurdity, and salacious accusations are automatically accepted as accurate, the number of quality people who risk their reputation to serve the country will continue to dwindle. What will remain is a group of people whose thirst for power and talent for bluster will overwhelm their sense of embarrassment from having their deficiencies exposed. Jeopardizing family, friends, and business interests cannot continue to be the cost of public service.

We must decide as to the type of people we want to run for elected office. If our frustration is centered on the quality of candidates, then it is incumbent upon us to create a political environment that is palatable for individuals with pure intentions. The ideal candidate is someone with a heart for service and a mind for policy, but anyone who possesses these skills is better compensated and fairly treated in private industry. We can improve our politics by recognizing that leaders have the same flaws as we do and that the best candidates are being dissuaded from participating in a process that seeks to expose weaknesses rather than applaud strengths. Before we criticize the political system in this country, we may want to examine the facets of dysfunction in which we have become active participants.

When our basic operational premise is that politicians are scoundrels, liars, and thieves, eventually we will create the conditions for those assumptions to come to fruition. By assuming the system is corrupt and the agents of our government are complicit, we leave no room for the blameless to distinguish themselves from the detestable. The current norm of making accusations and then searching for evidence until we prove our assertions is paradoxical to our stated goal of attaining adequate representation. Rather than allowing election-year mudslinging to remain an effective tool of manipulation, we should discourage the distortion of facts by taking it upon ourselves to analyze the résumé of a candidate instead of deferring to the accusations of their opponent. We stand on a compromised foundation when we plead for civility yet acquiesce to the normalization of deception and fail to recognize the power of truth in the voting process. We will not find the candidates who will serve our nation with distinction on the trash heap of our own rhetoric.

CHAPTER 38

Social Media

Social media platforms and applications were introduced with the expectation that they would bring people together and increase global connectivity. Each innovation allows users to maintain familial relationships and friendships no matter the distance, and enables business networks to evolve into financial transactions and economic engagement. Many of the supposed benefits have indeed come to fruition, but the simultaneous consequences of social media engagement threaten to negate the positive aspects of global networking. In the end, all the benefits pale in comparison to the toll social media use has on our ability to engage with the people in our households.

Interacting with a broad swath of the population is excellent, but it cannot be at the expense of our families. Every day billions of people wake up and obsessively check their social media profiles on a variety of platforms, and this habit is compulsively repeated until they lie down to sleep again at night. Moments that should remain in the private domain of the mind are instead filmed or photographed to be shared as a means to provide strangers a glimpse into our lives. Suddenly, memories are stored on the phone rather than enjoyed with a friend or loved one. Children are imprinted with the repeated task of staring into a camera instead of the eyes of a parent or caregiver. The memories are recorded, but the moment is lost to a common distraction that has corrupted our priorities and grown to dominate our existence.

Not only are we squandering life experiences by underestimating the extent of our infatuation, but we are also beginning to lose an entire generation of people to social media addiction. Treating our phones like a vital organ we need to survive is a problem that requires an immediate remedy, yet no one acknowledges the severity of our national obsession because it remains economically beneficial and yields sizable profits for some of the country's largest corporations. When families can go days without a genuine interaction with each other outside the scope of the technological engagement, it is indicative of a disease that is metastasizing without interference. The long-term success of our nation and the quality of life for its people depends on our ability to admit a problem exists and begin to devise a treatment that reintroduces the concept of being present in the moments happening in front of our eyes.

While we feel compelled to use social media every moment of the day, the companies that build the platforms are monetizing and exploiting our incessant need for acceptance and attention. They turn our addiction into billions of dollars and then make billions of dollars more when our data is sold or provided to strategic partners. We sell our souls for the opportunity to quench our thirst for contrived celebrity, and the companies immediately sell our collection of souls to the highest bidder. The erosion of intimate relationships and the relinquishment of our privacy are two transaction costs that are difficult to recoup in the digital age. Unfortunately, once we cede our identity to a screen, it is a near impossibility to regain control and retrieve all the time we have lost.

CHAPTER 39
Southern Border

The people who risk life and limb for a chance at the American Dream are not an invading force, but rather they are the best hope we have for a return to American exceptionalism. They have suffered the oppression of pseudodemocratic corruption and see the United States with the glimmer and zeal our citizenry has abandoned. They carry their children and the clothes on their back to make perilous journeys through cartel-infested cities where the local authorities are just as dangerous as the gang members they encounter at every turn. Despite the risk of starvation, brutal death, rape, or any other form of violence, they continue forward with the belief that hope resides on the other side of a fence or river in the desert. They cherish the ideals we used to appreciate, and they seek the life we now tell ourselves is a distant memory or a remnant of nationalistic folklore. For these immigrants, the opportunity for a better life for themselves and their children is a psychological and emotional force no legislative impediment or physical barrier can contain.

Immigration policy has become a tool for xenophobic expression, fraught with mischaracterizations that have led to a continually devolving intellectual discussion. The issue of allowing immigrants into the United States should not be a controversial topic controlled by the distribution of misinformation and widely accepted logical fallacies. Immigration should be tightly controlled to maintain a safe environment for economic and social stability, but the system must also be fair to those who wish to enter the country and pursue their American Dream. Immigrants from Mexico and Central America have arrived in the United States in droves for decades. While political debates have sought to create friction between citizens and immigrants, the reality is that millions of new residents have integrated seamlessly into the population and embraced the opportunities available in the United States. The present norm for a family arriving in the country, legally or illegally, includes finding employment, schools for their children, and adequate housing. The experience is similar to that of immigrants in the Northeast during the Industrial Revolution, yet in today's political climate, the influx of immigrants is characterized as dangerous instead of as a necessity that allows for dynamic economic growth. A declining birth rate and a deficit of labor resources compared to our global competitors cause new immigrants to be a valuable addition to the population. Immigrants arriving in the United States for nefarious purposes or engaging in illegal activities are the clear exception, not the rule, and should be treated as such.

It is essential to analyze the facts surrounding immigrants from Mexico and understand what makes them suitable for inclusion into the American population. Before considering the discrimination that exists because of their first language or skin color, they are a seemingly perfect fit for the value system that has traditionally characterized American power and exceptionalism. Immigrants hold hard work and family values in high regard. They are resourceful, ambitious, and enthusiastic about the opportunity to take full advantage of the economic opportunities in this country if given a chance to participate without fear of deportation or discrimination. The very political party that preaches the importance of traditional values is foolishly blind to the fact that this particular faction of immigrants and asylum seekers believe in the same set of ideological principles. In reality, increased immigration should be used as the standard for American policies that lead to a mutually beneficial outcome for all stakeholders. The fact that people from Mexico and Central America are subjected to the worst elements of xenophobic nationalism is indicative of the current political environment that encourages emotional reaction over reasonable consideration.

While immigrants from Mexico should be respected and allowed to transition into life as Americans, the problems at the southern border cannot be overlooked. However, border policy is not a protection mechanism for the American people alone. The future of border security must be considered from the perspective of both sides in the political debate. Safety for the residents in border states and the immigrants seeking to enter the United States are equally important objectives. Immigrants from Central America and Mexico who attempt to cross into the United States face perilous journeys. The routes to safety are controlled by cartels and corrupt government officials who use the helplessness and desperation of those seeking refuge to extort and abuse the innocent. The actions taken by human traffickers and cartel members are impossible to stop without implementing policy change in the United States that begins to streamline the immigration process for individuals and families who cannot afford to wait.

When discussing immigration through the southern border, it is counterproductive and illogical to villainize Mexican Americans or other immigrant groups. Our hostility and anger should instead be directed toward the embarrassingly corrupt political system in Mexico.

Our neighboring political leaders are manipulated and controlled by cartels and have become little more than an implicit partner in illegal and increasingly harmful activities. We must recognize that the families attempting to cross the border are running for their lives from a system that has implicitly endorsed lawlessness and refuses to protect fundamental human rights. Until the problems in the governments of Central America and Mexico are resolved, we must understand that the immigration problem is more similar to a refugee exodus from a drug-fueled banana republic. As much as Americans talk about human rights, it is disappointing to observe the lack of urgency for addressing the crisis that exists just beyond our southern border.

Complaining about current policy, prevailing attitudes, and rampant corruption is not enough to correct the problem. As the true nature of the crisis is revealed, the next step is to propose necessary reforms that will help alleviate the problem and combat the perpetuation of misinformation. The southern border represents a safety concern for American citizens and a humanitarian disaster for immigrant families. Because the issue is multifaceted, a detailed and articulate policy response is required. The border must be tightly controlled, but not through a wall symbolizing American belligerence instead of adequate security measures. Technological development will allow us to stem the flow of immigrants using routes controlled by drug cartels. The budgetary expense is sizable, but the action is not negotiable. As additional border agents and new surveillance technology are employed, the access points for immigrants must be improved and streamlined. Immigrants seeking entry to the United States must be able to arrive at various checkpoints along the border where they can submit their information for background checks and undergo basic health screenings for infectious diseases. Those who do not pass the background checks are denied entry, and individuals with health issues can be treated at clinics along the border before entering the country. We need to take back control of the border by making the process efficient and effective. When a family seeks refuge and economic opportunity in the United States, they should be able to arrive at a border intake office and be cleared for passage within twenty-four to forty-eight hours. An expedited and fair process for entry to this country will eliminate a significant revenue source for the cartels who charge exorbitant fees to smuggle families across the border.

Once an immigrant enters the United States, they will have the necessary paperwork from the border intake office and will be able to obtain the identification needed to drive, acquire housing, and find a job. Also, immigrant communities can be aided through existing social-service resources to learn how to find employment and begin the process of integration into the economy. In addition to providing paperwork and essential identification for new immigrants, it is vital to provide this service to individuals already inside the country. Without drivers' licenses or passports, current undocumented residents are vulnerable to abuse by law enforcement, government agencies, and employers, and they are less likely to report a crime for fear of deportation. The current state of fear millions of residents from Mexico and Central America face each day is not acceptable and should be considered a deterioration of our moral and ethical imperative to protect individuals and families in need of our help. The idea that we would take this group of people and make them a target of public ridicule is an utter embarrassment and a complete divergence from the foundational principles of our nation. The dream of immigrants is safety, security, economic prosperity, and access to excellent education, and it should be considered a violation of our social contract to restrict the promises of American prosperity without regard for the ambition of the human spirit. In America, we do not and cannot abandon our unique commitment to welcoming those who yearn to be free. If we extend the hand of protection, as has been the case for the entire history of our great nation, the immigrant population will become our greatest asset and the fuel for social, cultural, and economic innovation and progress.

CHAPTER 40
On Adversity

Poverty in the United States feels like an inescapable cycle of gaining a small step toward success and then being pushed back into the struggle before any momentum can be achieved. Poverty is not confined to resource scarcity. For the millions of people who struggle to survive each day, the burden is exhausting and erodes the physical, mental, and emotional health of the individual. Before a penny can be saved after a long week at work, something inevitably goes wrong and diminishes the will to push forward. Basic necessities feel like they are more expensive than they were the day before, and every problem becomes a suffocating crisis. This is the reality for many Americans who seek an education, a stable job, and an occasional helping hand, but they are instead met with condescension or entirely ignored.

Poverty is an enemy we need to defeat, but the adversity that is derived from hardship has proven to be a powerful force in shaping some of our greatest leaders. In reality, there is no way to guarantee scarce resources for all people, and life will always present difficult circumstances and challenges that must be met and overcome to achieve success. It is a testament to our economic system that many people avoid the burden of poverty or other economic limitations, but those who learn how to win in the face of defeat inspire us to push forward beyond our perceived limitations. When an individual does emerge from poverty, they are never asked about the tools they used to become successful. The assumption is that they had help, luck, or some type of advantage that caused them to defy the odds. We must continue working to bridge the gap of income inequality, but the lessons we learn in the midst of struggle are the forces that sharpen our focus and fuel our ambition. The people who emerge from their disadvantageous circumstances should be applauded for their will, and their perspective should be included as a resource so we can develop a holistic approach to poverty mitigation. Our experiences, paired with the means we have at our disposal, will create the conditions for the rising tide to lift all boats.

Adversity cannot be discounted as an important aspect of our development and something we all experience, regardless of our socioeconomic status. Poverty creates a divide between Americans based on their income, but overcoming adversity is something we all share in our pursuit of success. Let us embrace our shared experiences and work together to improve the lives of our fellow Americans. We are a stronger nation when we acknowledge the variety of ways in which we are all connected, and stop perpetuating a caste system that highlights our differences. "Nothing" is a difficult foundation on which to build an empire; therefore, the people who constantly manage to do so display innate characteristics that are enhanced through their circumstances and the adversity they overcome.

In actuality, adversity is a temporary hindrance for those who strive to achieve their goals. What we need to do as a country is not minimize or impugn the diverse experiences of our people, but rather make a greater effort to include those who do not come from a privileged background in the political and economic process. There remains no greater teacher than experience, so we should not castigate experiences frequently deemed inferior to others. Most aspects of competence and creativity cannot be learned in a classroom or listed on a résumé. It is important to provide tools that help those in poverty to emerge as successful examples of the American Dream, but it is not wise to diminish the role of the people facing suffocating socioeconomic conditions without any appreciation for the value they provide. Adversity is a teacher, and success is the diploma, and the incredible work ethic and ambition of the people who beat the odds inspire all of us to seek better futures for our families. The elimination of adversity sounds great as a mission statement for an organization or political platform, but it is an erosion of progressive development for those who emerge from the encumbrance of difficult circumstances focused on achieving success and creating a better America. We do not deserve the harvest unless we include those who toiled in the field and planted the seeds of national prosperity.

CHAPTER 41
Strategic Alliances

Strategic alliances are the lynchpins of global stability. The more that countries engage in effective communication and build sustained relationships, the more peaceful we can expect the geopolitical landscape to be for our children. Although leaders may come and go, each administration in the United States must be equally committed to policies that reinforce partnerships rather than alienate our friends around the world. The future will be built upon a foundation of mutually beneficial relationships that strive to solidify our commonalities and set aside, if only in critical moments, our differences.

A crucial aspect of formulating alliances for the future is to withhold the initial judgment of the nations with which we seek a relationship. Throughout the industrialized and developing world are despots and dictators who pose grave threats to the liberty of their people and the safety of their regions. While tolerating brutal and oppressive regimes is a direct contradiction to our sensibilities and cultural norms, a pathway for dialogue and diplomatic relations is always a preferable first step. Drawing redlines and offering empty threats of military intervention may exude strength at the moment, but years of inaction will begin to make such warnings counterproductive to the objectives at hand.

Additionally, the pressure of media or citizens with negligible understanding of the complexities surrounding geopolitical alliances should not become the arbiter of policies that affect the long-term safety and security of the United States. We should be accountable for missteps, but it is shortsighted to bow to pressure brought on by groups or individuals who are not privy to the full scope of relevant information. Tyrants become tyrannical when their absolute power is threatened or when they begin to feel impotent in the eyes of their people or neighboring countries. Exercising the brutish barbarism of a medieval lord is little more than the outburst of an emasculated child on the global stage. Such outbursts should be treated as such and ignored. Nothing is more inconsequential than the rambling tirade of a despot as their words fall on deaf ears. Let them build their crude weapons from the global scrapheap and focus on the development of alliances that render their titles useless outside of a United Nations conference room.

Too often, we base policy decisions on the perceived brutality of a dictator when they begin to threaten our freedom, yet we rarely mention the ruthlessness of the demure despot who refrains from advertising their atrocities. Foreign policy in this regard must be consistent to be effective. Either we are open to talks with any leader until they prove fruitless, or we remain steadfast in our belief that all leaders who oppress or harm their people should be isolated and left to their maniacal pursuit of interfering with global stability. The danger is not mitigated by excluding the dangerous, and crimes against humanity are exacerbated when tyrants are left to their own devices. We must do the hard work of building relationships that allow us to exert influence to protect the innocent.

The ultimate purpose of current and future alliances is to control or at least exercise significant influence over the evolution of strategic defense and economic growth in the age of globalization. The objective is to lead, and that requires reinforcing our traditional partnerships with neighbors and committed allies, but also forming new alliances with nations that threaten the safety and security of people and potential trade markets. Aligning ourselves with enemies of freedom is a difficult maneuver when the consequences of oppression are more evident with the power of social media, but we must approach global leadership with a long-term focus on the proliferation of peace rather than war. The most potent weapon in our arsenal is not to sacrifice American lives in an ill-advised war of attrition but rather to use the power of economic ties to suffocate tyranny with the threat of financial devastation. Trade, military, and diplomatic alliances do not exist to quell every conflict, but they are useful tools to mitigate the damages when disputes arise.

CHAPTER 42
Student Loans

The availability of ample student loans should have served as the solution to the chronic problem of higher-education access. Student loans provided by the federal government offer an opportunity for any person to attend college without consideration of their socioeconomic background or their ability to repay the loans upon graduation. The underlying belief is that a college education is an essential part of economic mobility and financial security for the individual and that the resulting degree will provide access to higher-paying jobs. As student-loan borrowers become gainfully employed with their new degrees, which they would have otherwise been unable to attain, they will then have the ability to begin repaying the loans. In a perfect world, student loans would be characterized as the catalyst for reducing, if not extinguishing, the inequality that plagues our nation. Instead, the idealistic vision of cognitive development and economic equality has become a nightmare of financial ruin that is on the verge of consuming the livelihoods of the very people the system intended to bolster.

The importance of a college degree has been diluted by the surplus of graduates in the job market who are underemployed and underpaid.

The dream of our parents and grandparents that the college degree would serve as the ticket for wealth and stability has diminished in a global economy in which the ability to adapt to a dynamic job market is more valuable than a diploma. Millions of college graduates aimlessly wait their turns in the queue for the opportunity to find out the extent to which they completely wasted their time in school exploring the nuances of eighteenth-century European poetry. Employers are increasingly in need of enthusiastic candidates with excellent interpersonal skills and a willingness to learn, and instead, they are faced with a generation of entitled graduates who have accepted the false notion of educational superiority and now demand a high wage and flexible hours before their student loan payments begin. Every degree cannot be of value when everyone has a degree.

Colleges must also be held accountable for the increasing burden of student debt. Colleges have exploited the new revenue source that the increased access to the student loan system has created. They have become a business, consumed with the political power and prominence that is generated by enrollment, and they have left the indebted students to fend for themselves. Colleges fully understand that the global economic system is not fueled by the monotonous memorization and regurgitation that has become the standard in higher education. Students in a four-year program are paying tuition rates that increase each year, yet the value received for those tuition dollars is dwindling. Additionally, after four years or more of hard work, a graduate realizes that most positions do not require any of the knowledge they gained in college, and even the jobs that do require or relate to a college degree incorporate extensive new-hire training programs that could have been taken by a high school graduate and filled the same function with equal competence.

The student-loan debt burden also continues to rise because colleges have used the additional revenue from higher tuition rates and

increased fees to bolster their images. The universities create new programs, new schools, and new colleges without sufficient evidence that
the programs they already offer are meeting the needs of the students
and potential employers. The new programs require new faculty, new
buildings, and new resources, and the administrators operate under
the assumption that future college students will accept their antiquated economic assumptions. Institutions of higher education must be
held accountable for justifying price increases by selling necessity, while
the number of graduates experiencing financial hardship from student
loans continues to rise. Increased access to financial aid is not intended
to serve as a pricing model for administrators, where even the most mediocre institutions creep purposefully toward the goal of having their
tuition match the maximum borrowing levels for federal student aid.

We must also consider the ethical responsibility universities should
have for their students when the value or cost of their product is called
into question. Currently, we have an environment where millions of
students barely entering adulthood have the opportunity to compromise their financial future in pursuit of hope instead of a tangible benefit. Students are falling prey to their fear of failure in the eyes of their
family or peers, and colleges are all too happy to monopolize on that
fear for their financial benefit. Instead of permitting the continued exploitation of youthful ignorance, we should insist that universities take
a leading role in educating students not only in the classroom, but also
on the tremendous consequences that result from paying exorbitant
educational costs with student loans they will be unlikely to afford
upon graduation. Students must be empowered to decide whether a
college degree is required for them to reach their full potential without
being scolded for daring to step outside the bounds of conventional
wisdom and make a decision guided by reason rather than unrealistic
assumptions. Sharing the truth that college degrees have a fluctuating

value in the global economy is the least we can do as student loan debt slowly erodes the foundation of personal finance. Eventually, this crisis may cause our economy to falter under the weight of declining optimism among a majority of working-class Americans.

As higher numbers of student loans are required to complete degrees, there is a significant diminishing return on the investment for the poverty-stricken Americans who were supposed to be freed from the chains of economic oppression by the availability of loans. Those in poverty have the most to lose from the increasing burden of high tuition and climbing loan balances because they lack the family financial resources to compensate for any lapses in employment or other possible hardships. In reality, people in poverty have been used as the symbol of educational virtue, while the powerful interests in higher education have used the circumstances to enrich themselves and their institutions. Those in poverty, who are supposedly at the forefront of policy considerations, have been disregarded and forgotten, while the growing albatross of debt is permanently affixed to their credit history and ensures that no amount of hard work will allow them to overcome their new financial reality.

Students loans and other forms of financial aid are a vital resource if used responsibly, but that responsibility does not lie singularly with the young man or woman seeking an education. Colleges have an equal responsibility to maintain reasonable tuition rates that allow their graduates to gain a strong financial foothold and flourish as educated adults. The current path of maximizing student debt regardless of the return on investment displays an intentional dereliction of ethical duty. Without a significant alteration of current borrowing patterns and tuition hikes, the marginalized people who should experience the most significant benefit of access to higher education will only become further marginalized. Alternatively, individuals with economic resources to withstand oppressive levels of debt accumulation will survive the turmoil of early adulthood and reap the greatest benefits. The ability to learn and think critically is the most valuable asset an individual can possess, but it cannot be appropriately fostered in a university classroom if it requires a student to accept financial servitude in exchange for a degree.

CHAPTER 43
On Religion

Few things can be more superfluous than to ponder eternity when common decency is the origin of social and cultural cohesion. In politics, resource allocation, and the development of community identity, religion has increasingly caused the ideological divide to deepen. The fundamental objective of mutually guaranteed peace and prosperity is never in greater peril than when religious leaders or politicians soaked in dogmatic platitudes seek to serve perverted interests in the name of spiritual obedience. Throughout history, the tattered remnants of human cooperation have been marred by the brutality of righteousness. Therefore, the prognosis for our future prosperity hinges on our ability to apply reason as a means to distinguish faith from ignorance and solve complex problems or reconcile tradition with progress.

The frailty of the religious foundation we stand upon is evident. Churches have built their own economies from a clearly defined threat of damnation and in turn provided a path to salvation through financial, spiritual, physical, and political dedication to the values extolled by faith-based organizations. The power of ideology is exemplified by the vast swaths of evangelicals who believe billions of people in each generation are subjected to eternal fire upon their death, yet their only misdeed was being born outside the sphere of partisan zealotry. The passionate pursuit of salvation has obscured the outright absurdity of the alternative outcome for the remaining majority of humanity.

Critical analysis of religion has no pertinence to the existence of God. Rather than questioning the immense personal benefit of individual spirituality, it is far more important to examine the value of the moral constructs that have been erected to the detriment of personal and collective liberty. Religious principles are amended opportunistically by leaders who seek to retain their relevance amid social and cultural evolution, yet they provide no such flexibility to the people who are subjected to the arbitrary enforcement of church dogma. Members of a religion are expected to continue following the antiquated virtues of yesteryear while the church leaders devise new iterations of truth to satisfy the emerging preferences of the next generation. The underlying dichotomy is the pursuit of absolute truth versus absolute extinction, and in times of change or crisis, a religion will always revise the truth to delay its demise. Absolute truth is only valuable when it engenders obedience from followers and leverage over detractors; therefore, when its power diminishes over time, the solution is always the imposition of a new absolute truth that adapts to modern sensibilities.

Religion will continue to be a powerful influence as long as the origin of our existence continues to evade the curious; however, the animosity within the warring factions of the worship industry must subside. No religion benefits from mutually assured destruction, no person benefits from the purposeful exploitation of faith, and no country is led to the promised land following the heretic with the mouth of a zealot. The best path to reverse the perversion of God is to respect the growing diversity of spirituality and resist the urge to demand absolute belief at the possible risk of eliminating the remnants of faith. Just as in the case of partisan politics, the truth exists in the vast chasm between absolutism and relativism. Unfortunately for the prominent religions that capitalize in a variety of ways on the fear of the unknown, the God-given gift of a sound mind will slowly prevail and upend their self-aggrandizing perversion of the most solemn practice.

CHAPTER 44
Taxes and Business

Every hardworking individual in the United States deserves to keep more of the money they rightfully earn. Residents of this country would rather use their income to support their families, help those in need, establish sufficient savings for retirement, and leave legacies for their children. The successful procurement of the American Dream should not become a measurement of greed that disallows the right a person has to the spoils of their effort. It is particularly outside the bounds of liberty and common sense for political leaders in a free nation to determine who is deserving of their own money. The money we have is a measure of our hard work, not the amount a government has decided we deserve. While the spending habits of the wealthy are typically easier to attack because their purchases are beyond our means, we are not made a penny richer when we admonish the successful for enjoying the fruits of their labor. Alternatively, it is unlikely that if we measured and examined the spending habits of low-income Americans, we would suddenly find the source of virtue in their bank statement. Appealing to our natural proclivity for jealousy and covetousness by presenting asymmetric information about the wealthiest Americans is intended to stir the rage and unrest that politicians claim they want to alleviate.

Before a successful business owner ever pays a dime in taxes, they will undertake the most challenging task in the American economy. Each entrepreneur risks financial ruin for themselves and their family to pursue little more than an idea. The pursuit is not based on a desire for fame and fortune, but rather the opportunity to be released from the financial and career limitations of corporate America and endeavor to find their unique niche in the economy. For many business owners, especially considering that a vast majority own and operate small businesses, this journey ends in failure many times before it finally yields a profit. Once a company finally begins to show a glimmer of possibility, a significant portion of income is poured into development and employees, and into building the necessary infrastructure to scale the business to the point where revenue is stable. Still, even at this point in the life cycle of the business, an owner faces the daily possibility of personal ruin if one vendor falls through, a single check arrives late, or a key employee decides to quit on a whim. Financial security in business is never assured, but as the revenue increases, it only serves as a minor reprieve from the new daily endeavor of working tirelessly to prevent everything from collapsing. At this point, politicians often begin to make assumptions of a business owner's deservedness based on the vehicle parked in front of their office building, or the home someone risked everything to afford. The political leaders who hunger for the earnings of others to sustain their power have little regard for the process of repeated sacrifice that is required to build a successful company with a sustainable profit margin. The revenue stream they covet is fueled by the sleepless nights and unending days of a person with the entrepreneurial spirit and the persistence to succeed.

Another overlooked facet of tax policy is the plethora of additional fees businesses must pay in addition to corporate and personal taxes to the federal government. In the throes of success, all hands want their opportunity to raid the cookie jar. Successful business owners who comply with every tax law pay corporate, personal, payroll, sales, capital gains, state, and local taxes. Additionally, the rates for required insurances and licenses increase as the business grows. The result of expanding revenue is not additional employees and public policies that support growth but rather a stomach-churning avalanche of bureaucratic interference and counterintuitive tax policies. Tax season should be the time Americans happily contribute toward the public good and infrastructure maintenance, but the oppressive nature of current policies from cities up to the federal government frequently leave the successful searching for any way to thwart the confiscation of their earnings. We should not place a burden so heavy on business owners that they begin to wonder if success is worth the pain and frustration.

Differentiating between the rich and the poor is the fallacy of the ill-informed. Those who have no idea how wealth is created are the first to propose the confiscation of income for redistribution, yet no one is made whole except politicians who gain power and influence by promising to strengthen the social safety net on the backs of the prosperous working class. Tax policy should consider the plight of the poor and the substantial risks taken by the wealthy to attain their status. The pocketbooks of the haves should no longer be used to buy the votes of the have-nots.

Fairness in tax policy is not achieved by increasing the burden on the rich. A fair tax is one that requires a proportional contribution from every American worker with increasing incentives as businesses and skilled employees experience higher revenues or wages. Our goal should be the inclusion of all income and elimination of tax havens and hidden income as an enthusiastic choice instead of a legal threat. Members of Congress need to understand and appreciate the sacrifices millions of Americans make to earn their prosperity and stop using anecdotal examples of poor money management or expensive severance packages to instigate conflict between employees and employers. The significant portion of wealth in the United States is held by Americans concerned for the plight of the less fortunate and who undertake significant philanthropic efforts to provide aid and job opportunities so all people can achieve their goals with hard work and perseverance.

An entirely new approach to taxes needs to be adopted to serve collective interests. State and local governments are happy to accommodate large corporations who seek favorable tax exemptions when they expand, but those same leaders discount the economic impact of the small businesses that together generate equal employment and investment outcomes. If a city or state can afford to eliminate taxes for a corporation, then they should consider having the same appreciation for the local businesses that are far more likely to thrive in their community and provide economic benefits. Additionally, federal policy must move beyond political strategy and the instigation of class warfare to find a balance between redistribution and creating an environment that encourages people of all income and education levels to be entrepreneurial and strive to meet their potential. Compelling Americans to compensate for fiscal mismanagement is the folly of leaders who are unable to see beyond their next election. Convincing those who are struggling to make ends meet that the wealthy are the cause of their shortfall is an absurd logical fallacy that seeks to shift blame away from those who deserve to be held responsible for such a grievance. In the end, tax policy should remain an intellectual discussion based on economic theory, not an ideological tool intended to deepen the political divide.

CHAPTER 45
Term Limits

Implementing term limits has become a fashionable idea among political candidates seeking to quell the fear of corruption among the general public. The proposal has merit if we consider the numerous candidates and elected officials who have become intent on making public service a career. For politicians throughout the United States, they operate under the assumption that their status as an incumbent allows abysmal loyalty to their constituents to go unnoticed. As long as a candidate maintains their party affiliation in heavily skewed districts, the likelihood of being defeated in an election is relatively small. If term limits are implemented, more candidates who would typically forgo running for public office would, in theory, have a fairer opportunity to be elected. When politicians have less time to ingratiate themselves in the corrupting influence of power and privilege, they will spend more time effectively representing the people of their states or districts.

Term limits are an attractive option for the millions of Americans frustrated by the deceit pervasive in politics and believe limiting political careers will help leaders remained focused and productive. Once again, a proposal, in theory, is not necessarily guaranteed to yield the intended result. Frustration and anger over the bickering and lack of productivity in government is a typical response from voters, but the appeal of good intentions should not cause us to abandon the institutions of our political system. Professional politicians are a stomach-churning source of platitudes and lies, but the real enemy of the people is the normalization of corruption as a means of executing the business of government. If the underlying system remains undisturbed, any candidate who wins an election will be subjected to the same procedures and expectations if they want to achieve any semblance of success for their constituents. It may be convenient to point toward an individual as the source of the problem, but the unfortunate reality is that the public scapegoat never represents the actual perpetrators of corruption.

The insistence on term limits also fails to recognize or appreciate the positive aspects of having experienced public servants. If a politician fails to meet the expectations of their voters, they can be defeated at the ballot box, but there is no reason to create an arbitrary mechanism to sweep all leaders, regardless of merit or skill, out of office to soothe our shortsighted demand for change. Would anyone tolerate being arbitrarily removed from their job after several years with no cause or justification? Additionally, what would be the effect on quality and productivity if a new employee was regularly replacing experienced and highly skilled staff? While we may not always approve of the outcome, and even despise the process, we should not disregard the value of having people in office who are experienced and skilled at administering the functions of government.

The introduction of term limits also assumes that such action would encourage more individuals to seek elected office and serve their communities. Unfortunately, in the system where powerful political parties serve as the architects of choice, there remain few opportunities for candidates outside the political elite to emerge as viable contenders.

Term limits will only serve as the engine of the modern political carrousel from which carefully selected candidates emerge from the assembly line to take their turn at the seat of power. If the same predetermined individuals who pass the litmus test of the major parties continue to be our only options, what is actually achieved by having a new name on the ballot every few years? Term limits should remain the job of an informed citizenry who acts at the voting booth to hold ineffective politicians accountable. A poorly constructed policy that sweeps our best leaders out of office along with the bad is little more than an example of our collective laziness when it comes to actively choosing who best represents our interests.

If we are waiting on the savior of Washington, we may not want to hold our breath. Instead, we must acknowledge that government is immensely complex, and having experienced public servants who win elections is not a violation of our liberties that must be amended. The best defense against perceived tyranny remains at the ballot box, and there should be no shortcuts that remove our responsibility as citizens to do our public duty and make wise choices among the myriad of candidates in each election. If we do our job, it will be sufficient to make sure our elected leaders do theirs as well.

CHAPTER 46
On Skepticism

Maintaining healthy skepticism is a mental exercise that supports daily introspection, and it must be applied in equal measure to all new information. We tend to accept data that supports our political identity or ideological preference and castigate sources that are deemed an attack on the beliefs we assume to be true. To better synthesize new information in political discourse, we need to grasp the extent of our own latent bias. Intellectual honesty and opportunities for personal growth stem from our ability to filter information through the lens of truth, not ideological harmony.

Accepting new information and the possible political, social, and cultural consequences of intellectual evolution is a positive activity for curious individuals who understand that the concepts and theories available for our consumption are inherently incomplete. A supposed fact from the past in any context can fade to obscurity when it is found to be incorrect, so it would be folly to assume the ideological principles that compose the foundations of our current beliefs are impenetrable. The task at hand is to begin building a cognitive framework based on critical analysis rather than strict adherence. Truth always seems like a righteous crusade until it is consumed by the advancement of knowledge and becomes merely a disputed relic of misguided observations kept alive by our self-centered quest to be right. To be right and factual are not always complementary endeavors when the truth is evident and exists independently and contrary to our intense desire to be correct.

Skepticism is also required because of the constant effort to filter information before it is presented to the general public. While journalists and scholars are essential contributors to information discovery, they are not above the innate human desire to be right. We search for answers to our questions, yet those that we choose to explore are carefully selected and crafted according to our ideological preferences. In the business of maximizing scarce resources, time is of the essence, and even the selection of what will be presented as news in the scope of our limited attention span is a decision driven by ideology. If the news were strictly presented in order of importance, would it not begin each day with the latest information on human suffering and progress in descending order until it arrived at our daily political disagreements? Instead, the information we see is arranged according to the questions we choose to pursue and the topics that will pique the curiosity of a general public consumed by chaos and dramatization. Skepticism and awareness will allow us to identify questionable information and the methods employed to distribute news laced in varying degrees with the political biases of the writer. We should not discount the importance of objective journalism and research, but we cannot abandon skepticism in search of news and opinions that validate our perspectives.

CHAPTER 47
Trade

Trade is generally viewed as a strictly financial transaction, but in reality, the tentacles of influence derived from trade agreements have far broader implications. Trade deficits and the proliferation of free trade agreements have significant economic impact in the context of globalization, but we cannot refrain from exploring the ancillary benefits that may help determine the direction of future policy decisions. With each trade agreement that is signed, we become intertwined in a complex relationship of influence, prosperity, and cooperation. It is shortsighted to analyze the value of our trade relationships based on a spreadsheet comprised of imports and exports that fails to account for the variables that make economic ties so crucial for the future of our nation.

A global community is only achieved when peace is more profitable than war. Therefore, our efforts must be directed at forging new partnerships and strengthening those that we have already secured. The trade imbalance is a problem that must be addressed reasonably, but in the end, it pales in comparison to the imbalance of human rights and economic opportunity that can be slowly remedied through mutually beneficial trade agreements. We must first understand that our intentions reach beyond the simplicity of a financial transaction with another nation. Unmitigated trade with countries from every corner of the globe provides greater security for our prosperity and stability. The establishment of a financially reinforced hierarchy offers a clearly defined concept of global leadership where we can cement our place as a world power for generations to come.

Additionally, trade can become a useful weapon in of itself. When new economic powers emerge to challenge the capitalist system, we will have the broad reach of our economic ties to resist the onslaught of tyrannical dictatorships draped in the trappings of the free-market system we established. If we suddenly embrace frugality amid a generational shift in global power, we risk alienating the trade partners who have committed to supporting our position in the geopolitical hierarchy. As economies around the world seek investments to achieve full-scale industrialization and maximum productivity, trade alliances will become equally as important as military alliances in securing the safety of our people and the sustainability of our capitalistic and democratic system.

Allowing unfettered access to the economic system of the United States will provide substantial benefits to people around the globe. More importantly, it will slowly erode the absolute power of corrupt regimes, which are currently dissuaded from market participation by the ambiguous sensibilities that influence our trade policy. Trading with despots is a stomach-churning calculation, but it is already standard operating procedure when it suits our economic needs. The fundamental difference between China and North Korea is that we willingly turn a blind eye to the human rights violations and geopolitical manipulation of one and readily express our dismay at the brutality of the other. Rather than being guided by the whims of a contrived morality, we should rely on our rational pragmatism to determine the best course of action.

CHAPTER 48
Welfare

Government assistance to those in poverty is an investment in the sustainability of our economic system. Without the aid, capitalism would be marred by the existence of pervasive scarcity, and the attitude of concerned citizens would turn from enthusiastic support of free markets to a preference for a more equitable economic theory. Although capitalism provides incredible mobility and prosperity for millions of people, millions more require assistance to maintain a basic quality of life. Subsidies are a positive form a redistribution that compensates for disparities in wealth and opportunity. Closing the gap between indigence and abundance is a crucial function of our government, and it allows families to sustain themselves with a baseline of financial assistance while they work toward more fruitful participation in our economic system.

Poverty alleviation is essential, but our government continues to uphold an unnecessarily paternalistic model of resource distribution. To assume poverty is an indicator of inferior intelligence, laziness, or financial mismanagement is also to promulgate the destructive presuppositions from the past. For a majority, government assistance serves as a helpful resource during times of transition, and where generational dependence exists, the likely causes are economic or cultural impediments that have yet to be remediated in our society. Blaming the poor for their condition or choosing to impugn their character with no knowledge of their specific circumstances is a destructive path political leaders should avoid if their intention is help develop a permanent solution to the problem.

Efficiency in the distribution of assistance has always been a chief concern of taxpayers and politicians. If we genuinely want to achieve the mission of providing aid to the poor in an efficient manner, the paternalistic foundation should be reconsidered. Rather than having dozens of programs at both the state and federal level functioning below their optimal performance, the funds contributed toward all assistance programs should be transitioned into a single payment system where the same amount of money is loaded onto a debit card for the individuals and families to decide the best use of their funds. A plethora of programs working simultaneously toward the same broad objective impedes optimization and limits the ability for the individual to allocate their funds effectively. Additionally, for the people facing challenging circumstances who are in need of the assistance, forcing them to search for various forms of aid and wade through a variety of applications is the antithesis of efficiency and concern for their well-being.

Poverty affects us all to varying degrees, and we must navigate a path through the ideological hostility to understand the plight of the suffering neighbor yearning for a brighter future. Those in poverty need kindness and understanding, not condescension and disrespect, because if we provide a stable foundation, a generation of people will be able to emerge from their financial conditions and succeed despite their temporary economic status. Each time we feel the urge to revert to our partisan battle lines and demand policies that reinforce implicit paternalism, we should remember that people, not statistics, are the topic of conversation. Making direct payments to those in poverty may not resolve every underlying issue that causes resource scarcity, but it will provide greater autonomy to the families in need. On the road to a better life, you cannot buy gas with food stamps.

CHAPTER 49
On Voting

Voting in each election is our civic duty as citizens of the United States, but casting our ballot represents only one step in the process of political engagement. We all voice our displeasure at the state of our government, but we refuse to take ownership of the central role we play in the slow erosion of our democracy. The name and brand recognition of candidates have taken the place of integrity and intelligence. We have happily delegated our right to choose representatives who reflect our values to corporations and wealthy donors who know that party affiliation and general appeal, not policy, are the main determinants of electability.

Democracy cannot be maintained when the average voters do not know the names of the people who have been entrusted to represent our priorities and secure a prosperous future for our children. Activism should be a device employed to prevent the destruction of our government, not a tool of reaction when the time to voice our frustration through voting has passed. A real activist does not take to the streets but instead wages a campaign of knowledge in their community to learn about the candidates who request their vote each election cycle.

Candidates and voters alike must take ownership of their shortcomings and admit the current condition of our political system is the result of our ignorance and not the fault of villainous straw men. We lack the initiative to engage with our political system aside from elections, and before protests are required, and the result is a collective discontent that pulls apart the social and cultural fabric of our nation.

The solution to regaining control of our government is simple. Those with power and influence who seek to manipulate voter turnout and nudge individuals toward a particular candidate can be defeated if we merely take it upon ourselves to learn the functions of government and the roles our representatives play in the direction of our country. Everyone should be encouraged to vote when they have the opportunity, but blindly casting a ballot for a candidate is a perversion of civic duty. However, the answer is not to abstain from choosing a representative who will enact our will; it is instead incumbent upon us to listen to their words, know their name, analyze their experience, and make a determination of fitness for political office intuitively and intelligently. We no longer have to be victims of our political system if we take the time to understand our role in controlling outcomes. Being informed about our system of government and each candidate is a far better alternative than an aimless political revolution. Our system is ideally suited for actively engaged citizens to make a determination of qualifications for every candidate who requests our support.

CHAPTER 50
Women's Rights

Equality for women in our society is no small task, due in large part to the impediments put in place by men who have enjoyed the security of dominance for the majority of human history. Advocating for an egalitarian society where gender roles are relegated to the past, and all people are celebrated for their unique skills and abilities, independent of their biological characteristics, is a cause worthy of our attention and support. While much progress has been made to create opportunities for women in all facets of life, there remain miles to go on this journey of enlightenment.

Beyond the voices of protest and demands for change, there must also be a series of specific actions that allow the objectives of the women's rights movement to supplant the traditional definition of female roles in the home, in the community, and the economy. Unfortunately, the most significant obstacle that remains is the attitude of men who feel threatened by the presence of successful and opinionated women. Objectification and belittlement are destructive defense mechanisms that allow men facing their own inadequacy to project their frailties onto someone else. The classroom, the workplace, and any space in between should become an environment where men and women can share their experiences and diverse knowledge to form a productive partnership pursuing mutually beneficial goals.

Men must overcome the belief that women require the protection of a paternalistic society to flourish. The core reason a woman would need protection is that men are allowed, and even encouraged, to view women as sexual objects whose value lies in their reproductive prowess or the services they can provide to a man. There is no special protection needed in a society in which men do not reduce themselves to the mentality of beasts and lose all semblance of respect and control over their behavior. Sexual violence must be eradicated so that this generation of women can be the first to walk down the street without fear or hesitation. Women are not asking for special treatment—only the same treatment and considerations men already provide to other men. Demanding equality and insisting that men's kindness be free of ulterior motives is not an affront to masculinity or the role of men in society. Such a request is merely an effort to gain a seat at the table of power and influence, therefore allowing women to take the lead in creating a new definition of gender roles that will enable our children to exist in a world we could only wish for today.

The future can be filled with incredible change and equal opportunity for all people, or we can maintain the soft tyranny of inequality masquerading as tradition. Why would anyone grant themselves the power to dictate the future of another, and what right do they have to expect our obedience in the continuation of norms we had no part in constructing? Every woman deserves to have mentors, colleagues, teachers, and friends who respect their intelligence rather than their sexuality and praise their strengths before referring to their weaknesses. Ultimately, we are all truly the same, filled with fear and hope, all the while working feverishly to conceal the many faults beneath the surface. Instead of using our commonalities to heal the ailments of the human condition, we prefer to create victims and enemies where they do not exist. Women do not need men to help them succeed, but instead, they request we kindly step aside and allow them to blaze their own path toward a genderless meritocracy.

Conclusion

There are no conclusions to draw, only thoughts to ponder. Using critical thinking to analyze the political, economic, and social predicament of our time does not require us to reach consensus, but it does insist that we use our collective experiences to push forward. It is lovely to imagine the life we want, but at a certain point, we must live in the reality that exists. The human experience is filled with a full range of emotions, successes, and hardships, but there is no reason why all of our shortcomings must become the central theme of our rhetoric. The best path forward is not to dwell on all of the failures, but rather to embrace each success as a step toward progress. No society has existed without fault, and we are no exception. The unique aspect of the American experiment is that we accept our deficiencies and remain steadfast in the belief that our strengths are sufficient to carry us forward.

The political debate has reached a fever pitch, and our only options are either mutually assured destruction or a renewed commitment to compromise. We all have issues that we believe should not be subjected to concessions, but if we treat our political opponents with the respect they deserve, we will find that concessions are the catalysts to productive policy development. It may feel in the moment as though our voice is heard when it is the loudest, but over time, we will find that a well-formulated opinion based on facts is a more reasonable method for affecting the direction of our country. All the consternation of this generation has only proven that dysfunction has no bounds. Alternatively, intelligent discussion and peaceful advocacy, if tried, will be the remedy for dissatisfaction and stagnation. Righteous indignation is not always unfounded, but when people close their minds to new information and refuse to heed the perspective of another, all issues suddenly become subject to the rigidity of ideological fervor.

We have become divided because of the desire to protect our artificially constructed sensibilities. The foundation of our discourse should never be to defeat our opponents, but rather to engage in thoughtful debate without losing an appreciation for our ideological foes. Despite our best efforts to propel every niche issue to the forefront of the national consciousness, the only issue that matters is our survival as a country. We can remain the example of liberty, tolerance, and prosperity in this most critical geopolitical era, or we can retreat into a primitive dystopia in which success is abandoned for jealousy and rage. There is no moral high ground to be gained in stripping away our decency in the name of change. We all want to expose the flaws in one another without taking inventory of our contribution to the national malaise in which we find ourselves.

The path we have yet to explore is to enhance our own lives by uplifting others and to accentuate our talents by allowing others to flourish. We are all equipped to contribute to society beyond comprehension if we encourage each other to embrace what makes us different. For it is the sum of our differences that make us a whole nation. There is no respect in division and no progress that can be achieved when we walk backward in search of absolution. Our political differences do not need to be ignored, but they cannot be used to destroy our common goal to maximize the positive impact of our existence.

If ideology were as important as we claim, then we would make a better effort to live it as often as we say it. Instead, it has become a societal wedge that creates a chasm within our own families. The antirevolution of ideological temperance would allow us to begin the process of healing divisions and mending the relationships required for us all to succeed. In the end, all reasonable Americans seek to secure the same terms. We want a safe environment for our children, the freedom of personal and political autonomy, and the opportunity to succeed without discrimination. These ideals should serve as our common bond and do not belong to a singular ideology or political party, but instead are a unique by-product of our social contract and the economic system that provides the upward mobility we seek.

The future is bright because while our political discourse has dissolved into a daily barrage of absurdity, we still express the true identity of our politics in the way we interact with each other regularly. Each day the media attempts to stir the discontent needed for ratings and clicks, but we all go about our lives with a sincere appreciation for the people with whom we share our human experience. We treat our neighbors, coworkers, and strangers as equals, and no artificial conflict will dissuade us from persisting in our daily habits of decency. We must remember that when our conversations turn from personal to political, ultimately, we are creating enemies out of our friends in the name of party loyalty and ideological allegiance. When we have that moment of reckoning with our behavior, we need to consider whether or not our political opinions were, in fact, more important than the human connections we cast aside. The straw man is an easy nemesis to defeat, but our ability to engage in intelligent discussion is only eroded when we use our imaginations to create enemies that do not exist.

Moderation is becoming an increasingly enticing alternative to political rivalry and mutually destructive rhetoric. The state of our discourse has eroded the common bond to the point where the appetite for polarization is waning. The reality today is that political dysfunction and unsubstantiated accusations control the flow of candidates and the reins of power, but the model is unsustainable. What is coming is a new era of American politics in which compromise is the norm and well-articulated ideas become the focus of policy development. A new day, as spring appears after a long winter, will emerge with a renewed sense of hope and appreciation for constructive debate. We currently feel powerless to stymie the normalization of hate and rage, but one voter at a time, reason will eventually prevail over irrationality.